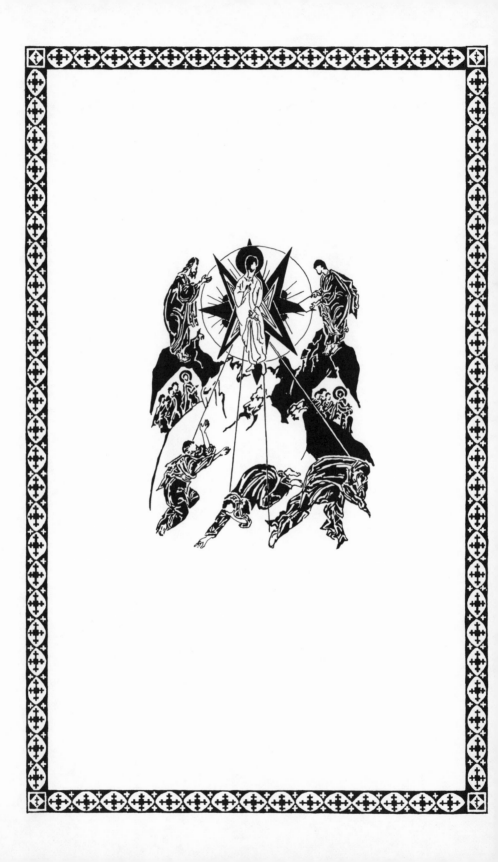

TRANSFIGURATION
of OUR LORD and SAVIOUR JESUS CHRIST

by

JOSEPH RAYA

former
Archbishop of Akka,
Haifa, Nazareth and
all Galilee

MADONNA HOUSE PUBLICATIONS

PUBLISHER: MADONNA HOUSE PUBLICATIONS
COMBERMERE, ONTARIO
CANADA K0J 1L0
ART: HEIDI HART
PHOTOGRAPHY: MR. GEORGE ONUSKA

Canadian Cataloguing in Publication Data
Raya, Joseph M.
  TRANSFIGURATION

ISBN 0-921440-29-4 bound
ISBN 0-921440-30-8 paperback

  1. Jesus Christ--Transfiguration. 2. Feast of the
Transfiguration. 3. Catholic Church--Byzantine rite.
I. Title.

BT410.R39 1992   232.9.'56   C92-090168-9

HIDDEN BUT REAL

*To Mary Davis, my faithful and untiring secretary,
my thanks!*

*To Reverend Deacon Robert Probert who has created for
this book an atmosphere of clarity and dignity. To Lois, his
wife and their son Paul, our appreciation and gratitude.*

My readers and I love to dwell in beauty.

Archbishop Joseph Raya

CONTENTS

MOSAIC OF THE
TRANSFIGURATION

TRANSFIGURATION CATHEDRAL
MARKHAM, ONT.

DEDICATION

THE *Transfiguration Cathedral of the Slovak Byzantine Church in Markham, Ontario is an expression of the dream of an immigrant who became one of the leading industrialists of Canada.*

Stephen Roman immigrated into Canada in the late 1930's. He carried as sole baggage an ardent intelligence, the heart of a child and the vision of a prophet. Love of family, of his Slovak Byzantine Church, and of both lands, the Slovak that raised him, and of Canada that adopted him, carried him to the highest summit of success.

Together with his bishop, Most Reverend Michael Rusnak, Stephen decided to share the magnificence of his church's tradition not only with his Slovak people but with all of Canada. He created a place for pilgrimage, and a centre of radiance of the beauty of the Transfiguration of Christ, our King and God. The Cathedral he offered is of Byzantine style, what historians of architecture call "the miracle in space" and "the supernatural creation of architecture".

The golden domes on the outside signify that the sphere of heaven has alighted on earth, and the icons and mosaics on the inside will send sparks of grandeur into our humanity to make every worshipper and every pilgrim sing for dignity, security and divine worth. Indeed, Byzantine worship is made to provide the worshipper with a feeling of nobility and freedom, not because of human voices and intellectual pronouncements, but because God is heard revealing the secrets of his love and summoning the human person to self-revelation.

Stephen Roman did not live long enough to see the complete realization of his dream. He nevertheless had the consolation to receive the Pope of Rome himself in his

Cathedral as one of the first pilgrims who stamped it with his approval and blessing.

In our Byzantine Church when Emperors, or great benefactors made such an offering to the people of God, a special portrait of them was included in the icon of Christ the Pantocrator. We hope that Stephen Roman will be represented like the Emperors of old, holding in his hands a miniature of his cathedral and offering it to Christ the King of all.

Now we offer You, our immortal Christ and God, this book as a first gift of thanks for his generosity:

"May his memory remain with us forever!"

A.R.

CATHEDRAL OF THE
TRANSFIGURATION
MARKHAM, ONT.

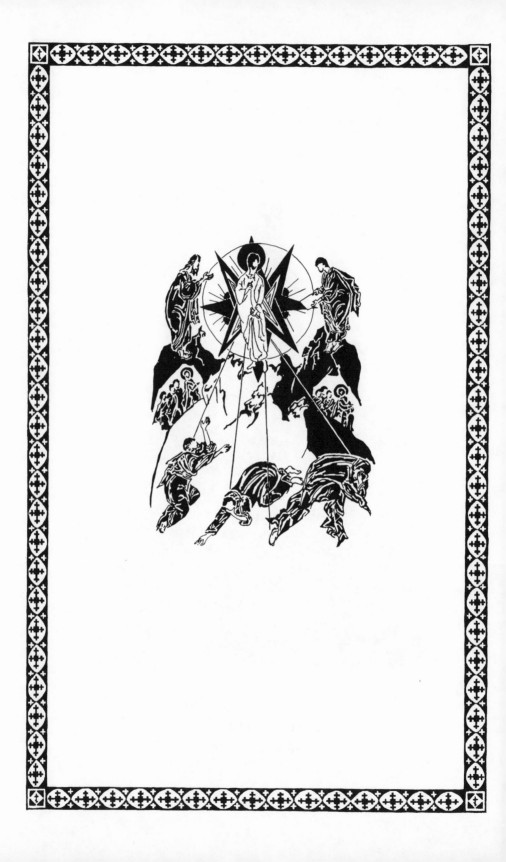

CHAPTER ONE

TRANSFIGURATION: MANIFESTATION OF GOD'S GLORY IN CHRIST

THE story of Transfiguration or manifestation of the divinity of Christ is related by three evangelists: Matthew, Mark, and Luke. All three of them tell the same story, and their accounts are almost identical.

Matthew says that the Lord, before he went up to Jerusalem to be crucified, took three of his disciples, Peter, James and John his brother, up

> *a high mountain where they could be alone.*
> *There in their presence, he was transfigured*
> > *(Matthew 17:1).*

Mark says,

> *Jesus took with him Peter and James and John ...*
> *in their presence he was transfigured (Mark 9:2).*

And Luke adds,

> *While he prayed his face was transfigured*
> *and his cloak became dazzling white (Luke 9:29).*

John does not mention the event.

GLORY OF GOD

THE word *transfigured*, as used by the Gospels, means a transformation in depth (metamorphosis). Our Blessed Lord appeared in a form surpassing in beauty the regular human form.   St. Matthew explains this type of transformation:

> *His face shone like the sun*
> *and his clothes became as dazzling white*
> *as light itself (Matthew 17:2).*

16

St Luke says,
> *While he prayed his face was transfigured*
> *and his cloak became dazzling white (Luke 9:29).*

And Mark explains further saying,
> *His clothes became dazzlingly white,*
> *whiter than any earthly bleacher could make them (Mark*
> *9:3).*

All these descriptions mean that Christ's divinity was made manifest and shone through his whole human make-up, in both his body and his raiment.

KENOSIS OF GOD

The story of Transfiguration illumines the meaning of the *Kenosis of God* and explains it. When he became man, our Lord and God Jesus Christ, the Son of God, the Only Begotten of the Father, the Light of Light, the One who is of one substance with the Father did not divest himself of his divinity, nor did he lose it. Neither did he abandon his humanity when he was transfigured. He did not submerge it in his divinity, nor did his divinity dissolve it. Transfiguration manifested plainly both divinity and humanity in Christ. Both divinity and humanity were apparent in him in glowing perfection. Divinity showed itself through the folds of his human skin, and his very clothes radiated it in all its divine reality.

Divinity was always present in Christ, even at the very moment of his Incarnation. St. John of Damascus says,

The body of Christ was glorified
[which really means divine]
since its very conception in the womb
in a way that the glory of the divinity
must have been also glory in his body.
Never was his divine body
separated from his divine glory.

Divinity was also present and real through all the events of his life, and no less present nor real during the moments of his suffering and burial. The historical Jesus Christ as he presents himself in the Gospels was God of God, true God of true God. Divinity was real and present in his human body as it was real in heaven in his divine person, in his unity with the Father and the Spirit.

The Incarnation of our Lord God and Saviour Jesus Christ, his nativity in Bethlehem, his circumcision on the eighth day, his presentation to the temple on the fortieth, and all the subsequent events of his earthly life demonstrate his *kenosis*.

Kenosis is a Greek word used by St. Paul to mean *emptiness*, a putting aside of a precious quality of being, and a temporary giving up of something intimately personal and gloriously exalting. When he became man the Son of God hid his divinity in the skin of our humanity. He did not lose it, nor renounce its presence in him, but covered it and lived as if it were not there.

This gesture of God was the expression of his most delicate thoughtfulness towards our humanity. We call this thoughtfulness *condescension*. Condescension of God does not mean *pity* a master has for an inferior, but the respect and consideration love inspires in the face of the frailty and personal limitations of the beloved one. When God the Son decided to come down to earth he did not appear in his glory and the brilliance of his divinity. The effulgence of his infinite glory would have blinded humanity and killed human sensitivity. God does not dazzle. He does not humiliate or embarrass humanity. He always seeks to identify with our own frailty and limitations. Therefore when he came down upon earth he chose to appear in a form we could understand and accept. He covered his divinity with the mantle of our skin, and the light of his dazzling glory with the smile of our human face. In order to enrich us and exalt us he put aside glory and divine brilliance to appear as a mere human like all of us.

For the sake of our human frailty and limitations Christ relinquished also other splendors of his divinity: his omnipotence, his divine omniscience, his omnipresence. Sometimes he even seems to have renounced consciousness of his divinity.

> *What an astonishing reality kenosis is!*
> *What respectful thoughtfulness our God has!*
> *This is pure love!!!*

In the fullness of love a person forgets himself or herself and gives himself or herself to the other in total self-surrender. And as our love cannot be real except to the extent to which we abandon ourselves, the Kenosis of God appears to be the supreme and unique example of perfect love!

In our human flesh God the Son observed and acted; he lived and died as any human being. So deeply and carefully hidden did our Lord keep his divinity from his contemporaries that every one of them thought that he was simply "the son of Joseph", the carpenter of Nazareth. Saint Matthew reports that people were saying,

*Where did this man get this wisdom
and these miraculous powers?*

*This is the carpenter's son, surely?
Is not his mother the woman called Mary,
and his brothers James and Joseph
and Simon and Jude?*

*His sisters, too, are they not all here with us?
So where did the man get it all (Matthew 13: 54-56).*

St. Paul called this attitude of the Lord *Kenosis*. He wrote,

*Christ's state was divine,
yet he did not cling
to his equality with God,*

*but emptied himself [Kenosis!]
To assume the condition of a slave,*

*and he became
as all men are (Phil. 2: 6-7).*

Upon recognizing this kenosis of God, St. Gregory of Nyssa exclaimed:

*If you had not hidden your divinity...
who would have been able
to sustain your glory?*

You came down, O Beautiful One,
in a form we can look at
and we can comprehend.

You came down
but you covered your divinity
with the mantle of our skin.

So deeply and preciously hidden did our Lord keep his divinity from his contemporaries! He manifested it only once, in a very private encounter with some of his disciples. And he urged them not to tell anyone about it until he rose from the dead. St. John Chrysostom explains:

God emptied himself
in order to draw us closer to him
and allow us to follow him
to the mountain of Tabor
where he showed himself to his disciples.

There he showed himself what he really was,
divine and essence of divinity.

Saint John of Damascus says again:
In his Transfiguration
Christ did not become what he was not before,
but he appeared to his apostles what he really was.
He opened their eyes, blind as they were to divinity,
giving them clear sight to see it
and to recognize him as he really was.

Christ allowed his disciples to experience divinity with their physical senses. Divine nature remained, naturally, inaccessible

21

in itself, but its energy and its internal glory were communicated to the created nature, to his body and to his clothing, and from there to the human eyes of his disciples to see. His material clothing was all radiant with divinity, and in this radiance divinity was somehow made visible. Through it the glory of the Uncreated God communicated itself to our humanity.

Tbe event on tbe mountain

SAINT Mark who wrote the Gospel known by his name was originally from Jerusalem. He was a disciple of the Lord and he helped Saint Paul in his missionary work. Later, he followed Saint Peter and became his constant companion and interpreter in Rome. He faithfully transcribed the preaching of his master for the people of Africa in Alexandria. His description of Transfiguration must be without a doubt the very words and intimate remembrance of Peter.

This is his story:

> *Six days later Jesus took with him Peter and James and John and led them up a high mountain where they could be alone by themselves. There in their presence he was transfigured: his clothes became dazzling white, whiter than any earthly bleacher could make them. Elijah appeared to them with Moses; and they were talking with Jesus. Then Peter spoke to Jesus: 'Rabbi,' he said, 'it is wonderful for us to be here; so let us make three tents, one for you, one for Moses and one for Elijah'.*

He did not know what to say;
they were so frightened.
And a cloud came, covering them in shadow;
and there came a voice from the cloud, 'This
is my Son, the Beloved. Listen to him.'
Then suddenly, when they looked around,
they saw no one with them anymore but only
Jesus (Mark 9: 2-8).

In Eastern theology and tradition, Transfiguration is an historical event as concrete as any human happening. Christ our Lord and the two prophets, Moses and Elijah, who appeared beside him, were not shadows in heaven, nor figures of someone's imagination, nor images seen in a dream. They were all physically present to each other, conversing with each other. Moreover, the three of them were also present and real to the disciples, who saw their faces and heard them speak. Christ, the two prophets, and the three disciples were perfectly aware of each other and of what was being said and done.

Throughout his entire life, Saint Peter was steeped in every detail of the event. He talks about it with a tremendous force and assurance in his second epistle.

It was not any cleverly invented myths
that we were repeating
when we brought you the knowledge
of the power and the coming of our Lord
Jesus Christ;

We had seen his majesty for ourselves.

He was honoured and glorified by
God the Father,

when the Sublime Glory itself
spoke to him and said,
'This is my Son, the Beloved;
He enjoys my favour.'

We heard this ourselves,
spoken from heaven,
when we were with him on the holy
mountain (2 Peter 1: 16-18).

Obviously, an eyewitness account of a real, life-transforming event!

REVELATION AT CAESAREA PHILIPPI

IN Saint Matthew there is a special preamble to the event of Transfiguration. St. Matthew tells of a trip for pleasure made by Christ to Caesarea Philippi which was indeed at that time, as it is still in our present day, a place for rest and relaxation, a national park for people's festivities and merry encounters.

Amid their festive activities, in a private conversation, Our Lord asked his disciples what the world thought of him: *"Who do people say the Son of Man is?"* he asked. The disciples answered, *"Some say that you are John the Baptist, some Elijah, and others Jeremiah, or one of the prophets"* *(Matthew 16:13,14).*

Naturally, the world judges by appearances. What the eyes had seen in Christ, what the ears had heard, and what the intelligence had discovered was his humanity. What the world realized first was that Christ was a real man, a man like all his contemporaries. But because of his miracles, and his sublime teaching, they suspected in him a greater spiritual quality yet, which they thought could make him equal to the great prophets Jeremiah, or Elijah, or other messengers of God.

Christ tried to draw the apostles closer to his real self by asking again what they themselves thought of him. The answer of the world as they reported it was not the real answer. There was something else more profound and more important our Lord wanted to challenge them to discover. He prodded them again. *"But you, who do you say I am?"*

Simon, son of Jonah, in a surge of loving enthusiasm answered for himself, and probably also for his fellow disciples who may have been saying it in a whisper among themselves *"You are the Christ, the Son of the living God ...."* The Lord said to him, *"Blessed are you, Simon bar Jonah, for flesh and blood have not revealed this to you, but my Father who is in heaven."* And to reward him for his insight the Lord changed his name from Simon to Peter: *"and I tell you, you are Peter [a rock] and on this rock I will build my church and the powers of death shall not prevail against it" (Matthew 16: 17-19).*

REVELATION THROUGH THE NAME

$\mathcal{I}$N Hebrew tradition, as in our Christian mentality, the name of a person represents the person who carries it. "In the name of God" means God himself. The Name *Hachem* (in Hebrew) means *God himself,* real and present. The name also designates the role the person is supposed to perform in life. For instance: *Yahweh* means the *One Who Is; Christ* means *The Anointed; Christopher* means *Christ Bearer; Abram* means *Wanderer;* etc. Even common names that designate specific trades become proper names when they identify persons by the role they play in life. Thus the one who makes bread is a *Baker*. He who works iron is a *Smith*, and he who tends sheep is a *Shepherd*.

In our Judeo-Christian holy books and cultures, when someone's role in life changes, his name is changed also to indicate the new role in life he or she has assumed. Thus when Abram, which means *the wanderer*, received God as a guest in his tent, he became his friend. So he was called *Abraham*, which means precisely *friend of God*. Jacob, after his struggle with the angel, became *Israel*, which means *the struggler with God*. Saul after his conversion to Christ became *Paul* the disciple; and Simon, after he recognized Christ to be *the Son of God*, became *Peter*, the *Rock*.

When we are baptized and receive the sacraments of Initiation, namely Baptism, Confirmation and Holy Eucharist, we become special members in the family of the Triune God. We receive a personal name that tells of our special spiritual quest in life. We call it a *Christian name*.

And when, later on in life, we happen to enter the service of the church in a religious order, we change our Christian name given us at baptism to a new name which will signify the new direction in life, or the new role we aim to achieve during the rest of our life as religious. We call it our *religious name*. Thus the one whose Church called *Joseph* at baptism becomes in religious life for example, *Christopher*. *Christopher*'s aim is now to *carry Christ*. The one who was endowed at Baptism with the quest to imitate Joseph in his silent dedication and so to bring about the Kingdom of God becomes someone whose aim in life is to carry Christ in his brother or sister. His quest in life is now to treat every human person as a brother or sister with the special motto:

My brother or my sister is my life.
My brother or sister is my joy!

Consider also the origin of Peter's name. At the time of Christ, Caesarea Philippi was a town built at the foot of a sheer rock, shining like a polished mirror in the sun. From under the rock a small river of clear water still springs out and forms the first source of the river Jordan. When Simon bar Jonah confessed that Christ is the Son of God, our Blessed Lord looked at the rock and told him that he is like that rock, in Greek, *Petra.* He even went a step further and identified Simon with it, telling him that he is that very rock, a *Petros* upon which he intended to build his Church. Just as no storm has ever prevailed against that rock of Caesarea Philippi, no power of hell can ever overcome his Church in Petros.

Good as it was, the confession of Simon Peter was still very far from expressing the whole truth about the personality of Christ. In reality, Christ was greater than the Messiah and more truly *Son of God,* than the expression meant in the mouth of the Apostles. Indeed, at the time of Christ, this appellation was a popular expression which meant simply a person who had a special relationship with God. Thus Israel was called *Son of God.* Special holy persons were also called *sons of God.*

Taking this opportunity of the confession of Peter, our Lord Jesus Christ decided to reveal fully the real meaning of the expression. He decided to reveal his divine nature. Christ was *The Son of God;* he was *God of God, Light of Light, true God of true God.* He was God himself manifested in our human flesh. God had manifested himself in the Old Testament in a dream-like way but at Transfiguration he manifested himself in all his divine reality. Our humanity overflowed with the radiance of his divinity allowing our very eyes to see him and to experience the beatitude of his beauty.

From among twelve Apostles the Lord chose only three, Peter, James and John to be witnesses of his Transfiguration because they were to be present at his agony in Gethsemane, and to witness the shame of human despair he would be plunged into upon his betrayal by Judas. In his infinite, loving thoughtfulness he wanted to protect them from discouragement when they would see him in such a state. This experience of his divine reality prepared them to bear the shame of his forthcoming apparent defeat and humiliation. Only because they saw his divine reality would they remember and not lose heart; only because they saw his divine glory could they become the witnesses of his suffering and death and understand his Resurrection. The liturgy echoes this intention of the Lord again and again:

> *Peter, James and John were present*
> *because they were to be with you*
> *at the time of Judas' betrayal,*
>
> *So that having seen you in glory*
> *they would remember*
> *and not be dismayed*
> *at the time of your suffering (Vespers).*

The liturgy repeats again and again the same theme for our own benefit, so that we too will remember and not be scandalized by the horrors of the Lord's suffering.

> *O Lord, as a preparation to your crucifixion,*
> *you led some of your disciples*
> *to a high mountain.*
>
> *Peter, James and John were present,*

28

the same three who were to be with you
at the time of Judas' betrayal.

So that having seen you in glory
they would not be dismayed
at the time of your suffering.

Likewise, O Lord, make us worthy
to recognize you as our God
and to adore you (Vespers).

And again:

O Christ God, you were transfigured on the mountain
and your disciples saw
as much of your glory
as they could behold,

So that seeing you crucified
they would know
you had willed to suffer passion
and would proclaim to the world
that you are verily the reflection of the Father.

Both evangelists Matthew and Mark begin their accounts of the Transfiguration with a reference to that previous incident in Caesarea Philippi by saying,

"Six days later [after that incident]
... Jesus took Peter, James and John, his brother,
and led them up a high mountain apart,
and he was transfigured before them."

The words: "Six days later...." allude to the story of Exodus where the glory of God remained on the mountain for six days before God appeared to Moses. The writers of the New Testament are always conscious of the continuity between the Old and the New Testament. As there was a period of six days between the revelation of the glory of God and his manifestation to Moses, so there was a six day period between the declaration of Peter and the personal manifestation of Christ's divinity.

This is the story to which the holy Gospel alludes:

When Moses went up on the mountain,
a cloud covered the mountain,
and the glory of the Lord settled on Mount Sinai.

For six days the cloud covered the mountain,
and on the seventh day the Lord called to Moses
from within the cloud.

To the Israelites the glory of the Lord
looked like a consuming fire
on top of the mountain.

Then Moses entered the cloud
as he went on up the mountain.
And he stayed on the mountain
forty days and forty nights. (Ex. 24, 15-18)

This story and all similar stories of the Old Testament were constantly used by the Church to express that the God of the Old Testament who spoke to Moses and the Prophets is the same God who is now speaking to his apostles and friends Peter, James and John.

Thus for the Christian religion, the theophanies, or

manifestations of God experienced by Moses and later by Elijah, are the prototypes of the glory of God on Mount Tabor. The stories of past theophanies were so important in the eyes of Christianity that the Church included them in its offices of worship long before theologians composed their hymns and iconographers wrote their icons.

The glory of our Lord and God in his Transfiguration is more real yet and more personal than the glory Moses and Elijah contemplated in the Old Testament. For both Moses and Elijah, on Mount Sinai and on Mount Horeb respectively, God was a glimpse or a dream-like apparition. On Mount Tabor he was actually present in the physical make up of our humanity. Christ is thus the extension and continuation of God *Yahweh* himself.

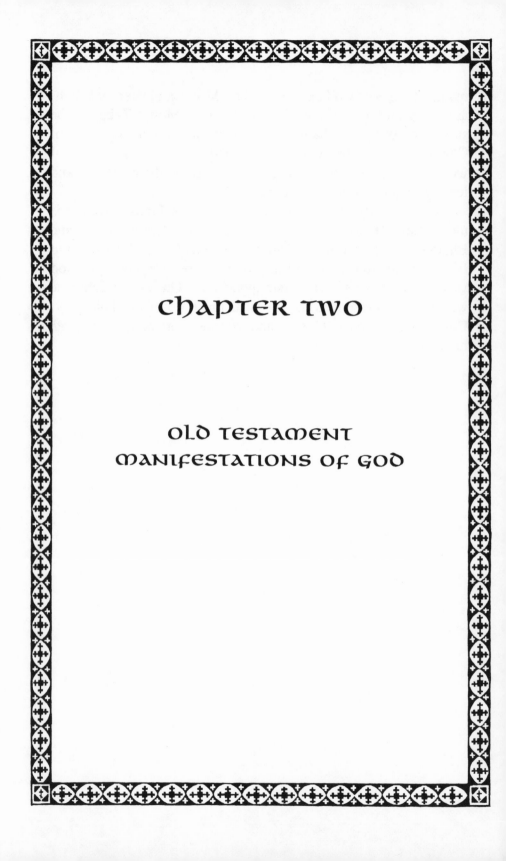

CHAPTER TWO

OLD TESTAMENT
MANIFESTATIONS OF GOD

THE first theme of the celebration of the feast of Transfiguration is that our Christian religion is the culmination and final fruition of the Old Testament history.

When the Church took upon itself the task of composing liturgies and celebrations for the benefit of the faithful, it looked first for ways to demonstrate that our religion was the continuation and realization of the plan of redemption that existed in God from all eternity. From his heart, redemption flowed into every detail of the history of mankind represented by the people of the Old Testament and marched along with Israel. Redemption was alive in every event of Old Testament history and was a song in every pronouncement of the Prophets. The Old Testament was the harbinger and herald of the redemption which found its fullness in our Lord and God Jesus Christ.

Consequently, our Christian religion was not the product of an accident of history, or the result of a new philosophy. Much less was it a movement of mere social reforms, or a reaction against the established Judaism. It was rather its continuation and fulfillment.

FIRST MANIFESTATION OF GOD TO MOSES

THE very first manifestation of God's glory was to Moses in the Burning Bush on Mount Horeb as reported in Exodus:

> *Moses led his flock*
> *to the far side of the wilderness*
> *and came to Horeb,*

the mountain of God.

There the angel of Yahweh
appeared to him
in the shape of a flame of fire,
coming from the middle of a bush.

Moses looked;
there was the bush blazing
but it was not being burnt up.

'I must go and look at this strange sight,'
Moses said
'and see why the bush is not burnt.'

Now Yahweh saw him go forward to look,
and God called to him
from the middle of the bush.
'Moses! Moses!' he said.

'Here I am' he answered.

'Come no nearer' he said.
'Take off your shoes,
for the place on which you stand
is holy ground.'

'I am the God of your father,' he said,
'the God of Abraham
the God of Isaac
and the God of Jacob.'

At this Moses covered his face,
afraid to look at God (Ex. 3: 1-6)

This manifestation is important for our Christian religion because it is also the symbol of many events of the New Testament in which the divinity of God is a fire that burns but does not consume and destroy. God, the burning fire, became a human being in the womb of a girl of our human race and did not consume her. So, we call Mary the "Burning Bush".

When we take in the Eucharist it is God we receive, the consuming fire, who comes to dwell in us without consuming us. After receiving him we pray,

> *O You who graciously*
> *give your flesh to me as food,*
> *You who are a fire*
> *consuming the unworthy,*
>
> *Consume me not, O my Creator.*
> *But rather pass through all the parts of my body,*
> *into all my joints,*
> *my heart, my soul.*
>
> *Burn, O good Lord,*
> *the thorns of my transgressions,*
> *cleanse my soul*
> *and purify all my thoughts....*

Thus, in holy communion we consider our human make up of body and soul as being in a "Burning Bush" where God resides in the fire of his divinity and does not consume us.
The vision of the bush is doubly important for us because it reveals also that God is a real person, with a personal name. He is so real that he is in constant relationship with his creation. He is alive and conscious of both the living and the dead:

Then Moses said to God,
'I am to go, then, to the sons
of Israel and say to them,
"The God of your Fathers
has sent me to you."

But if they ask me,
what his name is,
what am I to tell them?'

And God said to Moses,
'I Am who I Am.

This' he added, 'is what you must say
to the sons of Israel:
"I Am has sent me to you".

This is my Name for all time;
by this name I shall be invoked
for all generations to come' (Ex. 3: 13-15).

The holy Name of God, *I Am, Yahweh,* has been translated into our Church language by *O Aon*! All the icons of our Blessed Lord carry this name written in gold in the halo or in the nimbus around his face. It indicates the theological view expressed in the Creed that Christ, Son of God, is really and truly the very God of the Old Testament. He is *Son* which means of one substance with both the Father and the Holy Spirit, and he is ever present with us until the consummation of the world.

SECOND MANIFESTATION TO MOSES

IN its celebration of the Transfiguration of Christ on Mount Tabor the Church reads the story of the vision of Moses. We read first the manifestation to Moses as reported in Exodus: The Lord God said to Moses,

'Come up to me on the mountain,
and wait there;
and I will give you the tablets of stone,
with the law and the commandment,
which I have written for their instruction.'

So Moses rose with his servant Joshua,
and Moses went up unto the mountain of God.
He had said to the elders,
'Tarry here for us, until we come to you again;
and behold, Aaron and Hur are with you;
whoever has a cause, let him go to them.'

Then Moses went up on the mountain,
and the cloud covered the mountain.
The glory of the Lord settled on Mount Sinai,
and the cloud covered it six days;
and on the seventh day
he called to Moses out of the midst of the cloud.

Now the appearance of the glory of the Lord
was like a devouring fire on the top of the mountain
in the sight of the people of Israel.

And Moses entered the cloud,

and went up on the mountain.
And Moses was on the mountain forty days
and forty nights (Exodus 24:12-18).

Another experience of the vision of God, his third manifestation, was also that of Moses:

Thus the Lord used to speak to Moses
face to face, as a man speaks to his friend.
When Moses turned again into the camp,
his servant Joshua son of Nun,
a young man, did not depart from the tent.
Moses said to the Lord,
'See, You say to me, "Bring up this people;"
but you have not let me know whom
you will send with me.

Yet you have said "I know you by name,
and you have also found favour in my sight."
Now therefore, I pray you,
if I have found favour in your sight,
show me now your ways,
that I may know you and find favour in your sight.
Consider too that this nation is your people.'

And he said, 'I myself will go with you,
and I will give you rest.'

And he said to him,
'If your presence will not go with me,
do not carry us up from here.
For how shall it be known that

I have found favour in your sight,
I and your people?

Is it not in your going with us,
so that we are distinct,
I and your people,
from all other people
that are upon the face of the earth?'

And the Lord said to Moses,
'This very thing that you have spoken I will do;
for you have found favour in my sight
and I know you by name.'

Moses said, 'I pray you, show me your glory.'
And he said,
'I will make all my goodness pass before you,
and will proclaim before you my name The Lord
and I will be gracious to whom I will be gracious,
and will show mercy on whom I will show mercy.'

'But,' he said, 'you cannot see my face;
for man shall not see me and live.'

And the Lord said 'Behold, there is a place
by me where you shall stand upon the rock;
and while my glory passes by
I will put you in a cleft of the rock,
and I will cover you with my hand
until I have passed by;
then I will take away my hand,
and you shall see my back;
but my face shall not be seen.'

And Moses rose early in the morning
and went up on Mount Sinai,
as the Lord had commanded him
and took in his hand two tablets of stone.

And the Lord descended in a form of cloud
and stood with him there,
and proclaimed the name of the Lord.

The Lord passed before him,
and proclaimed, 'The Lord, the Lord,
a God merciful and gracious, slow to anger,
and abounding in steadfast love and faithfulness...'

And Moses made haste to bow his head toward the earth
and worshipped (Ex. 33: 11-23, 34: 4-8).

After all these manifestations to Moses, the glory of God took a dwelling place in the tent for the duration of the forty years of pilgrimage Moses lived in the desert:

When Moses entered the tent,
the pillar of cloud would descend
and stand at the door of the tent,
and the Lord would speak with Moses.

And when all the people saw the pillar of cloud
standing at the door of the tent,
all the people would rise up and worship,
every man at his tent door (Ex. 33: 9-10).

MANIFESTATION TO SOLOMON

FINALLY the glory of God was housed permanently in the temple Solomon built in Jerusalem as it is reported in 2 Chronicles:

> *When Solomon had finished his prayer,*
> *fire came down from heaven*
> *and consumed the holocaust*
> *and the sacrifices;*
>
> *And the glory of Yahweh*
> *filled the temple.*
> *The priests could not enter*
> *the house of Yahweh*
> *because the glory of Yahweh*
> *filled the house of Yahweh.*
>
> *All the sons of Israel,*
> *seeing the fire came down*
> *and the glory of God*
> *resting on the temple,*
> *bowed down on the pavement*
> *with their faces to the earth (2 Chronicles 7: 1-3).*

Inspired by these stories of the Old Testament, Peter volunteered to build a tent, a tabernacle, a temple, to house the "glory of God" on Mount Tabor as shown in the face of Our Lord. He aspired to have a permanent dwelling place for Christ to keep on shining forever. He said to the Lord:

Master, it is wonderful for us
to be here;
So, let us make three tents,
one for you, one for Moses, and one for Elijah
(Luke 9: 33).

Most probably, Peter had in mind a place like the Holy of
Holies, or other memorials of the Old Testament where the
luminous presence of God's glory had been permanent and
visible.

ᙏᗅNIᖴᘿᔕᎢᗅᎢIᝪN Ꭲᝪ ᘿᒪIᒍᗅᕼ

𝕿HE fourth experience of the vision of the glory of
God in the Old Testament was that of Elijah reported in the first
book of Kings:

And the Lord said 'Go forth,
and stand upon the mount before the Lord.'
And behold, the Lord passed by,
and a great and strong wind rent the mountains,
and broke in pieces the rocks before the Lord.

But the Lord was not in the wind;
and after the wind an earthquake,
but the Lord was not in the earthquake.

And after the earthquake a fire,
but the Lord was not in the fire.
And after the fire a still small voice.

And when Elijah heard it,

stood at the entrance of the cave.
And behold, there came a voice to him,
and said, 'What are you doing here Elijah?'
He said, 'I have been very jealous
for the Lord, the God of hosts;
for the people of Israel have forsaken your covenant,
thrown down your altars,
and slain your prophets with the sword;
and I, even I only, am left.'
And the Lord said to him,

'Go, return on your way
to the wilderness of Damascus:
and when you arrive, you shall... anoint
Elisha the Son of Shaphat of Abel-Meholah
to be prophet in your place' (1 Kings 19: 11-16).

These Theophanies of God to Moses, Elijah, and Solomon were *figures* - a foretaste of his real revelation face to face on Mount Tabor. God saw fit to prepare humanity through the events of the Old Testament for the fullness of his vision in the New, even as he warned Moses: "No one can see my face and stay alive".

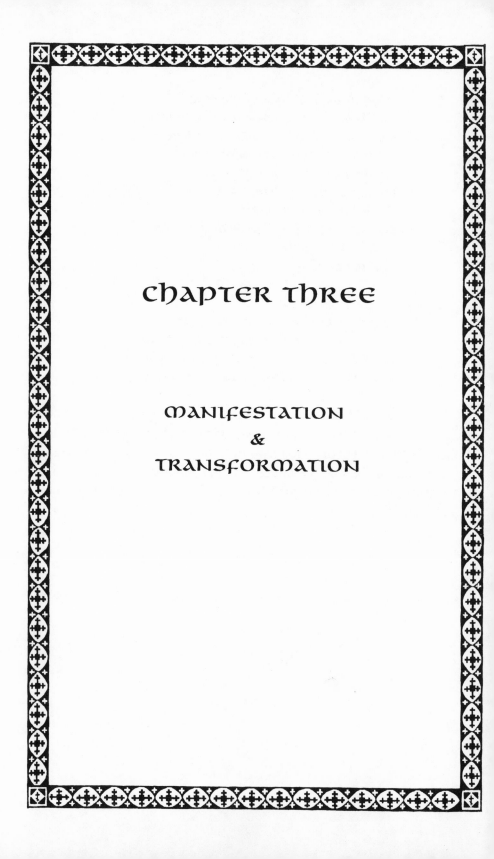

CHAPTER THREE

MANIFESTATION
&
TRANSFORMATION

$\mathfrak{I}$N the New Testament, humanity was able to see God. God manifested himself - divinity poured out of Christ's person and flooded humanity and humanity did not die. God was seen with human eyes aglow in the very make-up of our human flesh.

Saint Gregory of Nyssa remarks that "concepts of God create idols. Only amazement can comprehend something". The manifestation of God to the Apostles on Tabor was so much more amazing and glorious than all other visions of God that it made them admire and comprehend.

Transfiguration was the glory of God shining upon the earth, through the humanity of Christ, even through the very material of his clothing. It was the undreamed-of beatitude that showed how our human flesh had been soaked with divine glory and transfigured by God since the time of his Incarnation. As God's manifestation had transformed Moses in the Old Testament, so it transformed also the Apostles who saw his glory.

TRANSFORMATION OF MOSES

$\mathfrak{A}$FTER conversing with God Moses came down from Mount Sinai. His face was so bright and radiant that the people could not bear to look at him.

When Moses came down from Mount Sinai...
he did not know that the skin of his face
was radiant after speaking with Yahweh.

And when Aaron and all the sons of Israel
saw Moses, the skin on his face shone so much

that they would not venture near him.
And the sons of Israel would see
the face of Moses radiant.
Then Moses would put the veil back
over his face until he returned
to speak with Yahweh. (Ex. 34: 29-30,35)

TRANSFORMATION OF THE APOSTLES

LIKEWISE, on the Mount of Transfiguration, Christ shone with such radiance (*"brighter even than the sun"* say the Gospels) that the disciples could not bear to gaze directly at him. The intensity of the radiance of his divine presence swept them away and the brilliance of his beauty absorbed all their attention. They could not endure to think of any other thing, or see any other reality. They were in ecstasy.

Saint Luke expresses this ecstacy by the word *sleep.*

Peter and his companions were
  heavy with sleep,

But they kept awake
  and saw his glory
  and the two men standing with him (Luke 9:32).

The notion of *sleep* as mentioned here is admirably suited to express the disciples' experience of ecstasy in the presence of Christ. The immensity of his divine glory attracted all the powers of their faculties, synchronized and harmonized them into unity, and centered them on one unique object: Christ in glory. The disciples were completely oblivious of everything else. There is no better expression than the word *sleep* to describe such an intense concentration.

This *sleep* does not prevent one from being wide awake. And the Gospel goes on to say that "they kept awake". They were perfectly conscious. They saw and heard every one of the personages and understood well what was going on around them. The glory of Christ was of such intensity that nothing else could distract them from it. Their vision was not a speculative consideration, nor an hallucination, but a concrete experience thoroughly penetrated by the radiance of divinity. They were so absorbed, and so carried away by it, that nothing else mattered to them. They were heavy with sleep - yet fully aware of what was happening.

In his commentary on the Canticle of Canticles, St. Gregory of Nyssa explains the nature of such a "sleep" by saying *"The vision of God lulls to unconsciousness every bodily motion. The soul becomes able to receive the vision in a divine wakefulness, which is a pure and naked intuition of this loving presence."* And Gregory adds this wish:

May we make ourselves worthy of such a vision,
achieving by this sleep the awakening of our soul.

The liturgy of Transfiguration echoes this same wish at Vespers:

Let us receive light from his light,
and with radiant joy
let us forever sing
the praises of the consubstantial Trinity.

The vision of the manifestation of God is the perfect exemplification of what our mystical theology calls "illumination", or "beatific vision" of the face of Christ in heaven. The vision transforms into beatitude and ecstasy. It transformed not only Peter and John, but also transformed even the Evangelists who had not seen it, but had only heard about it second hand.

TRANSFORMATION OF PETER

TRANSFIGURATION seems to have transformed Peter's life into tranquility and peace. Later, when the vision was completed by the experience of the Resurrection of Christ, Peter's whole attitude became one of gentleness and radiance. To the end of his life he was vibrant with all the details of this experience. It made him humble and serene whenever he remembered it:

> *We had seen his majesty for ourselves.*
> *He was honored and glorified*
> *by God the Father,*
>
> *When the Sublime Glory itself*
> *spoke to him and said,*
> *'This is my Son, the Beloved;*
> *he enjoys my favor'.*
>
> *We heard this ourselves,*
> *spoken from heaven,*
> *When we were with him*
> *on the holy mountain. (2 Peter 1:17-18)*

TRANSFORMATION OF JOHN

OF the four Evangelists, John is the only one who was present at the event of the Transfiguration. He is also the only Evangelist who does not mention it in his Gospel. For him it was a reality of such spiritual grandeur that he could not mention it as a mere event or as a mere historical fact. After having witnessed it and thought about it, his whole being became alive with its light and glory. His Gospel and all his Epistles are stamped with the brilliance of the person of Christ, and with the grandeur of his divine glory.

Unlike Paul and the other Apostles, John saw all the events of the life of Christ not only as historical, but also as theological. For him these events flowered in time, but had their roots in eternity. John recorded the Christ of history, but as he had seen him in the glory of Transfiguration. For him Christ was Life and Light of the world. He was Nourishment for the hunger of mankind and Refreshment to quench its thirst:

All that came to be had life in him
and that Life was the Light of men,

A light that shines in the dark,
a light that darkness could not overpower.
(John 1: 4,5).

This last affirmation is only the echo of what John had heard and seen on the mountain. He makes Christ himself echo the reality of Tabor when he makes him declare *"I am the light of the world"* (John 9,5).

For John, Christ dissipates darkness and gloom and gives hope and joy. Christ is Life who gives *"life to any one he chooses"* (John 5:21). He is a refreshing Drink, "welling up to eternal life" (John 4: 14). He is the *"Bread of life",* and the Resurrection of all: "He who comes to me will never be hungry" *(John 6: 35).*

For John, Christ remains Light and Glory even at the time of his passion. Even in the midst of the immense humiliation of his crucifixion John makes Christ declare:

> *When I am lifted up*
> *from the earth,*
> *I shall draw to myself*
> *all humanity (John 12: 32).*

John's vision of Christ's glory and triumph does not falter even at the greatest moment of Our Lord's anguish:

> *Now the hour has come*
> *for the Son of man to be glorified.*
>
> *My soul is troubled.*
> *What shall I say:*
> *Father, save me from this hour?*
>
> *But it was for this very reason that*
> *I have come to this hour.*
>
> *Father, glorify your name! (John 12: 23,27-28)*

Immediately after these words of dismay John lets us hear the answer of the Father:

> *A voice came from heaven,*
> *'I have glorified it,*
> *and I will glorify it again'. (John 12: 28)*

Finally, Transfiguration seems to have turned John into a troubadour of love. All his life long he sang love, so much so that he was the only one among the disciples and apostles to deserve to be called *theologos,* singer of love, a theologian. At the end of his life he never tired of repeating to his disciples:

> *My dear children,*
> *let us love one another,*
> *because God is love.*
>
> *This is the love I mean,*
> *not our love for God,*
> *but God's love for us. (1 John 4:7,10)*

TRANSFORMATION OF THE OTHER EVANGELISTS

THE three other Evangelists who report the story of Transfiguration were not present at the event. They did not witness it. But they must have absorbed all these details and all the radiance of the face of Christ described to them. They tell with excitement and awe all the details they heard in whispers from Peter, John, and James as if they had been the ones present - as if they had been the ones who had seen with their own eyes what had happened.

All three of them seem to be at a loss for words to describe the event and everything involved in it. They all direct our attention to a most sacred and revealing fact. They all point to the *glory* of Christ.

"His face shone like the sun," says Matthew (17:2). *"His clothes became dazzlingly white,"* adds Mark. And he goes on

to stress his image by saying *"Whiter than any earthly bleacher could make them"* (Mark 9:3). Luke says, *"The aspect of his face was changed and his clothing became brilliant as lightning"* (Luke 9:29).

The words the Evangelists use to describe Christ's appearance in Transfiguration have a very specific meaning and significance in the vocabulary of the Bible and the language of the Fathers. Words such as "light", "dazzlingly white", "shining as the sun", are terms conveying images of divinity. Divinity appears to human contemplation as an ineffable reality that can only be approached by means of such expressions.

The light of Transfiguration was not a material light produced by sun or moon or stars, not an intellectual enlightenment, nor a meteorological phenomenon, but an Uncreated Light that had its source in God alone. As described in the Gospels, it can only be understood as emanating solely from God - eternal, infinite, uncircumscribed, and indefinable.

St. Gregory Palamas explains,

Sensible light shows things to our senses.
The intellectual light is to manifest the truth
which is contained in thoughts.
But those who receive the spiritual
or supernatural light,
perceive what is beyond all intellect.
They participate in the divine energies
and become themselves, in a sort, light.
When they unite to the Light
they see with it in full all that is hidden from those
who have not seen the grace of light.
The Uncreated Light
is the Light where God makes himself manifest

to those who enter into union with him.

The Uncreated Light exists in the inner sphere of the Trinity and cannot emanate but from the Trinity. It is a glory proper to Christ and to those who share divinization in Christ. The liturgy proclaims at Vespers:

> *He who mysteriously*
> *spoke to Moses on Mount Sinai*
> *and said: 'I am Who I am,'*
>
> *Today manifests himself*
> *to his disciples*
> *and reveals through his person*
> *that human nature*
> *is re-established in its original splendor.*

St. Maximos the Confessor explains: *"the light that shone out of the face of Christ is an emanation of divinity beyond expression, and larger than the infinite of infinity."*

GOSPEL NOTIONS OF DIVINITY:

LIGHT

All three Evangelists characterize the divinity of Christ as light and brilliance. The Fathers of the Church used the same word to describe Christ's divinity. They used also the words *splendor, beauty, theophany, power,* and *glory of the Father.* Oriental cultures, whether pagan or Judeo-Christian, use the same terminology to predicate the notion of divinity. Hinduism, Buddhism, as well as Iranian and Chinese religions, characterize divinity by the same words: *light* and *brilliance.*

Eastern, as well as Western liturgies are impregnated with prayers and expressions that carry the theme of light as describing the divinity of God. In the morning we sing to God the Father:

In your Light [who is Christ]
we shall see Light [the Holy Spirit]

At the first hour of the rising sun we pray:

O Christ, true Light,
who enlightens and sanctifies
every human person in this world
mark us with the light of your countenance,
that we may see the unapproachable radiance.

Let our life be straight
along the way of your commandments.

At vespers, when the light of day has waned, and darkness has prevailed, we pray again and we sing to Christ:

O gladsome Light!
Light and holy glory
of the Father immortal!

And when the mystery of mysteries has been received in the body and blood of Christ we proclaim:

We have seen the true Light!
We have received the heavenly Spirit
We have found the true faith.
We worship the undivided Trinity!
For Trinity has saved us.

Holy Saturday is called the Saturday of light. It is Christ Himself who is Light, from whom every light in the world, and every illumination takes reality and meaning, and in whom our divinization finds a bridal chamber illumined by the light of his face. Christ is proclaimed:

> *Source of life and immortality,*
> *eternal Light born of eternal Light,*
> *immortal Light, invisible, incomprehensible,*
>
> *You are the Light of the eternal Father's glory*
> *and its Radiance ...*
> *You are the Light of every human being*
> *who comes into this world.*

And the prayer continues to proclaim our divinization as light:

> *You filled our human nature*
> *with the light of your resurrection*
> *bestowing upon the world a new life*
> *and a new light brighter than the sun.*
>
> *Bestow this perfection of light upon us*
> *so that we may come with You*
> *into Your heavenly bridal chamber,*
> *to enjoy the light of the indivisible Trinity ....*

The first light of innocence and goodness that shone at the first creation is now seen shining in the face of Christ on Mount Tabor. It will shine again, and will be visible again in his Resurrection and in every human face at his second coming when everything will become new in him:

O You, who have spread
the first irradiation of light
to make all your works
sing in clarity,

O Christ, the Creator,
direct our ways to Your Light.

Of all the lights mentioned in holy Scripture as being manifestations of God's presence, the light of Transfiguration is considered to be the most sublime, because it unites the depth of vision on the part of man, and of effulgent revelation on the part of God. In it, man sees his divinization. In it also, God pours out into us the richness of his life.

Gregory of Nazianza writes:

Light was He who appeared to Moses in the burning bush
and the bush was not consumed.
Light was He who guided Israel in the column of fire
which made the harsh desert a sweet place to dwell in ....

Light was He who elevated Elijah on a chariot of fire
which did not consume the one who was sitting on it.

Light was He who illuminated the shepherds
all around with light,
when Light eternal made his appearance
in the light of this world.

Light was the brilliance of the star of Bethlehem
that guided the wise men, who offered their gifts,
to the Light who was born for us
and who became our Light.

*Light was the Divinity
that manifested itself to the disciples
on Mount Tabor....*

WHITENESS

The description of Transfiguration given by the Evangelists includes also the symbolism of *white* and *whiteness*. Matthew says, "his raiment was white as the light" (17:2). "And his raiment became shining, exceeding white as snow," says Mark (9:3). "And his raiment was white and glistening," says Luke (9:29).

The image of the whiteness of Christ's clothing is particularly rich in meaning. In Christian tradition, white vestments have always symbolized freedom, divine glory, and incorruptibility. Before their fall, Adam and Eve are said to have shared the glory of the "white robe of innocence". We believe also that on the last day when Christ will appear again, the just will put on the "white robe" of innocence and immortality. St. Athanasius of Sinai said:

> *He who had put on himself the sad skin of our humanity has donned a white vestment wrapped in light as with a mantle of Mount Tabor.*

At every baptism, we clothe the baptized with a white robe, and we sing, *"Give unto me a robe of light, O You who are clothed with light as with a garment ...."* The newly baptized is thus robed with a mantle of glory and immortality, the white robe of divinization. Likewise, the bride is dressed in white at her Crowning, as a sign and symbol of her freedom, and of her divine dignity and worth.

GLORY

Transfiguration has also been called the "manifestation of the glory of Christ".

Webster lists at least ten definitions of the word glory. Besides the usual synonyms, such as praise, honour, admiration, and honourable fame, glory has also been used to mean brilliancy, splendor, radiant beauty of a divine being, the manifestation of the divine nature, and favour to the blessed in heaven or celestial honour. It is also a term for heaven.

We also call the halo, or the nimbus of our Lord, of his blessed Mother, and that of the saints, *glory*. This is because it is a sign and symbol of the intense holiness that fills them with such an overflow that it radiates as a crown of glory around their heads. Heaven surrounds them, fills every fiber of their body and bursts out into splendor, forming a halo around their heads.

As a verb, glory means to exalt with joy or in triumph as in the expression "I glory in my progress". "I glory in my weakness", says St. Paul, "because of the grace of Christ who strengthens me."

Used in our Christian prayers, the word glory carries all these meanings. It also describes the acts of praise and honour we offer God, and the state of praising God, who is Brilliancy and radiant Beauty. Finally, the word glory points to the manifestation of the divine, and to the context in which the Kingdom of heaven can be recreated on earth. Glory is the key to the Kingdom.

The word glory was used in the Old Testament in many different ways. It meant first the respect due to God, and the feeling of awe one experiences in the presence of God. Later it was used for God himself, for the Invisible announcing his own presence in meteorological phenomena in the sky, in lightning and thunder, in the "smoke of mountains" (volcanos), and in the rushing of waters:

> *The voice of the Lord over the waters,*
> *the Lord over the multitudinous waters.*
>
> *The voice of the Lord in power!*
> *The voice of the Lord in splendor!*
> *The God of glory thunders.*
> *In his palace everything cries 'glory' (Ps. 29:3).*

Glory was also associated with the infinite goodness of God. "Heaven and earth are full of your glory!" (Is. 6,4). The knowledge of his glory creates the obligation to live according to his divine attributes of justice and generosity. Glory also meant the God who dwelled among his people as Liberator and Guide.

God is said to have "revealed in glory" his presence in order that all creation might recognize him, and in return offer him praise and honour. The human person in return is said to have been "crowned with honour and glory" and "set with all things under his feet" (Ps. 8:6). Because he is the image of God and the expression of his glory, the human person is indeed the priest of creation and its messenger before God. In him and through him creation speaks, and the universe finds a voice that can give glory.

For us Christians, Christ was, and will forever be, the perfect Singer of the glory of God. Glory is his personal attribute. Glorification and adoration found their purest expression in him. In him also, even repentance was complete adoration and glorification. He, the Innocent, made a perfect confession before God which no human person could ever have made for himself. St. Paul says: *"It was God's purpose to reveal... and to show all the rich glory of this mystery to pagans. The mystery is Christ among you, your hope of glory" (Col. 1:27).*

During his lifetime, Christ was the glory of God in healing the sick, the blind, and in raising the dead. The Evangelists always point out how people were taken by sentiments of awe and wonder at the sight of his miracles, and how they "glorified" God.

At his birth the Shepherds "glorified", says Luke. At his miracles people "glorified", say Luke and John. People "adored", say Mark and Matthew.

The misty breath of the Holy Spirit on the Mount of Transfiguration, the gush of light from Christ's clothes, the air resounding with the voice of the Father, and the heavens from above - every single detail of the Gospels' descriptions seems to sing the glory of Christ. Everything in this world is at the service of his glory. The glory of Christ is so immense, and so infinite, that no one can absorb all of its brilliance. The disciples could only behold a part of it, each according to his own capacity. We sing in the Troparion of the Feast:

> *When you were transfigured on the Mountain,*
> *O Christ our God,*
> *Your disciples beheld of your glory*
> *as much as they could bear ....*

And at the Lete we sing:

> *They saw as much as their bodily eyes*
> *were able to receive....*

At the Parousia, the whole glory of Christ will flood humanity and bathe it in brilliance and divine splendor!!!

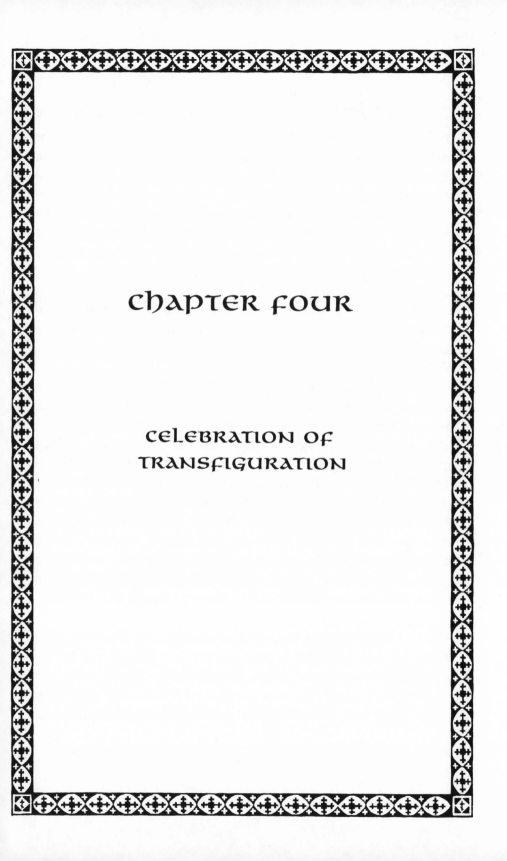

chapter four

celebration of transfiguration

CHRISTIAN religion was instituted by Christ to save the world, not by the logic of human intellect, nor by the wisdom of philosophy, but through the feast. Celebrating the feast is a participation in Christ and in the fullness of his life, a joy, a security, and a delight.

It is only in the feast that we can fully understand the reality of God, the meaning of both our salvation, and our divinization. It is in the feast also that we are able to contemplate spiritual realities, and enter into communion with God. In the feast theology blends with both liturgy and the icon to make our celebration the honourable place where heaven and earth meet. Theology proclaims what scripture and prayer have revealed, the liturgy sings it, and the icon writes it in colours and secret conversations.

In Eastern Tradition, theology, liturgy, and the icon are three expressions of the same, identical faith in the Triune God, and in Christ, our God who became man to divinize humanity and creation. Theology, liturgy, and the icon are a trilogy inspired by the Gospel and sustained by the light of Transfiguration. What theology contemplates, liturgy and icon proclaim. What theology cannot comprehend or explain, liturgy sings and the icon displays in beauty and elegance of silent movements. Theology, the icon, and liturgy all proclaim the same faith in the same worship. They differ only in their means of expression. Every sacrament and every truth of our Christian religion is for our Church a celebration of theological thinking, of poetry and of art.

Transfiguration is a feast of primary importance among all the feasts because it is a perfect exemplification of the theology of Incarnation, of the meaning of our divinization, and of the Christian teaching on the personal relationship that unites us to God and to each other. Theologians, liturgists and iconographers display a special interest in bringing out all the spiritual riches the feast contains.

Transfiguration is at the base, the starting point, of comprehending the difference between appearance and reality, between analyzing and contemplating, possessing and cherishing. Cherishing is life-giving, possessing transient; contemplation is a glory of relationship in love, analyzing a fleeting satisfaction of the mind; reality is more precious and more meaningful than any appearance. The theological themes of this feast are rich in spiritual, as well as in social consequences. We shall consider some of these themes and leave the other, more obvious ones, to personal meditation.

CELEBRATION OF CHRIST'S DIVINE PERSON

THE personal contact with the most wonderful wonder of God's divinity flowered in the Apostles into amazement and love - and they *understood* something special of their relationship with him. In such a relationship we can discover that we are loved and we can reciprocate love. In the personal encounter with his divine person, Christ raises us up from the finite limitation of our nature to his infinite glory. As the reflection of a face in clear water responds to our face, Christ reflects our own human face in the clean, clear water of his divinity. He showed us that he is the real Lover and we, his disciples, his beloved ones. In this personal encounter with the Lord Jesus Christ, we experience also that he was indeed, the "Bride", the "Everything" of our existence!

Set me like a seal on your heart,
like a seal on your arm.
For love is strong as Death,
jealously relentless as Sheol.

The flash of it is a flash of fire,
a flame of Yahweh himself.
(Canticles 8:6)

Transfiguration has been very popular since the beginning of the history of the Church. In the year 326, Helen, mother of Constantine the Great, the Roman Emperor, ordered a church to be built on Mount Tabor in Galilee, where tradition held that Transfiguration took place. The feast became more and more popular, not only in Palestine, but in Syria, in Egypt, and in far away Armenia. Saint Cyril of Jerusalem (c.348) mentions it in his catechesis (12,16).

At the end of the eighth century, or more probably in the ninth, the feast of Transfiguration was introduced in the Western church. But it was not until the year 1131 that the prestigious monastery of Cluny tried to popularize it in France. The Church of Rome adopted it officially in the year 1475, in commemoration of the victory Christian armies, led by John Hunyadi, had won over the Turks at Belgrade on July 22 of the year 1456.

All the feasts of the Church celebrate either an aspect of the personality of Christ or an event of his earthly life. Thus *Christmas* celebrates his birth and the *pilgrimming* of the universe to the place where he was born. His *Baptism* demonstrates his humility and the fact that he is One of the Trinity. *Resurrection* magnifies his triumph over death. *Transfiguration* celebrates him as a perfect God and a perfect man. It is the most dazzling event of his life because it is the spectacle of divinity appearing through the folds of our humanity. It is the Infinite who shows himself in the limits of our skin, and the Creator who enters into contact with his creation to fan the new flame of love that enlightens and unites. This is the undreamed-of truth that God is in love with us to the point of sharing with us the divine energies of his nature.

Transfiguration is also the celebration of our own divinization.

CELEBRATION OF OUR DIVINIZATION

BESIDES being the festival of *Light,* of *Brilliance,* of *Whiteness,* and of *Glory* (all names signifying divinity), Transfiguration is also the feast of beauty, of freedom, and of human dignity. From the brilliance of the face of Christ every human face, no matter how ugly and distorted it appears, acquires beauty, dignity, and divine worth. Transfiguration reveals the true meaning of divinization and shows the glorious outcome of our own life at the Parousia.

Contemplation of the beauty of Christ on Mount Tabor is the paradigm of our contemplation of the face of God in the beatific vision in heaven.

At Vespers we sing,

> *He who mysteriously spoke to Moses*
> *on Mount Sinai and said,*
> *I am Who I am!*
> *Today manifests himself to his disciples*
> *and reveals through his person*
> *that human nature*
> *is re-established in its original splendor.*

He made them witnesses
and partakers of this joy.
He raised up Moses and Elijah
the forerunners of the glorious
and Saving Resurrection
made possible by the Cross of Christ.

Divinization is not simply the image of God restored to its pristine beauty, it is our whole human reality made participant in God's trinitarian life, not of course in a formal similitude, but in a vital assimilation. Transfiguration is the celebration of our divinization. This gift of the Trinity consists of the divine energy of God communicated to us through the plenitude of divinity which is in Christ. Saint John declares that "Christ received the fullness of divinity, and from his plenitude we have all received."

Saint Basil says,

The prize of virtue is to become like God,
to be illumined with the purest light there is
in becoming children of that Day
that no darkness can obscure.

Once that Day has illumined us
he does not set down in the West any more,
but envelops everything with his luminous power,
and transforms into other Suns
all those who partake of him.

In other words we become by grace what God is by nature. This mystic reality is visible in the glorified body of Christ on Mount Tabor. As the red hot iron is not only transformed into fire, but radiates fire while itself remaining iron, so the human person is transfigured by divinization, with nothing of her or his humanity destroyed or taken away. In his or her inner reality the human person is all penetrated by the light of divinity, and made a sharer in Christ's glory while remaining holy human.

By penetrating our human nature, making it *divinity, light,* and *brilliance,* divinization gives us also a special power to live God's way of dealing with creation and with other persons. This was the meaning of the commandment of the Lord when he said, "Be ye all perfect as your Father in heaven is perfect" (Matt. 5:48). The perfection of God is not simply a moral quality of the avoidance of sin, but a positive outlook on love which he ordered to be without limit or condition. This special quality of love, says Saint John, was that of the Lord's. His love was "until the end" (Jn.13:1).

The first meaning of the expression "until the end" is the ultimate end or goal of love which is to give up one's own life in order that others can live. The Lord said, "There is no greater love than to give one's life for one's friends" (John 15: 13). The second meaning, which goes hand in hand with the first, and makes it perfect, is that this love is to be without limit or condition. This is *Theosis.*

Theosis is precisely that theological concept through which the Fathers and Byzantine theologians have explained the progress of the person toward divine similitude. It is the revelation which was given to Adam at creation and denied at the Fall, but it was followed to perfection by our Lord Jesus Christ.

This was the type of love Christ practiced. He united himself to a humanity which was unredeemed and in a state of sin. He never wavered in his love for it, carrying it from his Incarnation to the last breath of his life. He loved it to the end limit of love by laying down his own life and dying on the cross so that it might live.

This love was always without limit or condition. Christ forgave anyone who came in contact with him. He prayed for his own executioners who had rejected him and crucified him, and forgave them generously and spontaneously by asking the Father: "Father, forgive them; they do not know what they are doing" (Luke 23:34). And to all sinners he promised immediate entry into beatitude in the person of the thief, when he said to him, "I promise you, today you will be with me in Paradise" (Luke 23:43).

Christ who loved "until the end" wanted us, his followers, to practice the same type of love: "love one another as I have loved you!"

Such love cannot be conceived, and the command to love in such a way cannot be given, but by a divine Being. Moreover it cannot be practiced but by one who has been divinized. Only an infinite Intelligence can conceive and realize such a doctrine. The Lord was that infinite divinity who wanted his followers to be divine and to act and live divinely through theosis.

Divinization is life and the bestower of life. It dissipates darkness and transfigures everything into beatitude. It is clarity and order, truth and beauty. God is Light. Christ is the Emanation of light. And the Christian at his or her level is "light of the world" (Matthew 5:14).

Divinization is an awesome, mystical power no one individual can absorb in all its splendor nor put to work in all circumstances of life, but it can be measured in terms of our own personal spiritual stamina and strength. Each one receives and absorbs according to the measure of his or her ability. The hymns of the liturgy remind us again and again that our perception of God's glory, and consequently the depth of our life in him, depend on our level of spiritual strength, and psychological maturity and capability.

The Apostles are said to have seen of the glory of Christ, each one according to his capability:

They saw of your glory,
as much as they could bear.

They saw of him
as much as they could behold.
(Office of the feast)

Living our divinization does not rely on the observation of established laws and rules, nor on the mere submission to commandments. Rather, it is determined by our personal aptitude for compassion and caring, and our willingness to respond to the appeal of God.

CELEBRATION OF RENEWAL

TRANSFIGURATION is celebrated on August sixth as a feast of renewal. On that day the faithful bring to church the first fruits of the season. They offer them to God by sharing them with the community. The offering is a sign that the poor and the needy do not have to and will not have to worry about their subsistence. Those who have land and produce will give to those who do not. *Agape,* the brotherly love, is in full view.

In Holy Scripture, God orders that the first fruits of each season be offered to him as a sign that all the subsequent fruits belong also to him. Seeds are sown and they die in winter. They bloom in the spring and now, in summer, they start producing their first fruits. The fall will bring them to full maturity and abundance. God generously gives fruit and produce. Christians emulate the generosity of God with a generosity of their own. They choose the occasion of the feast of Transfiguration to demonstrate their concern and their love for each other.

Once Christians have recognized their dignity in divinization, as soon as the earth has yielded its first fruits, they offer them to God by sharing them with those who are in need. The liturgy sings:

> *O God with your radiance*
> *you sanctified the whole earth*
> *together with all its inhabitants.*
>
> *You were transfigured on a mountain*
> *and showed your might*
> *to your disciples.*
>
> *You have redeemed the world*
> *from transgression.*

The source of our Christian way of life is, indeed, the Transfiguration of Christ; it is the inner sanctuary of our relation with him. The teaching and actions of Christ as related in the Gospels are the focal point of our attention. Transfiguration fills us with wonder and surprises and stamps us with a stirring experience of life, allowing us to live it fully so that others can live it in the same intensity. The disciple of Christ is continually going deeper into the heart of the Lord, and into the beatitudes of the Gospel to extract more tenderness and more generosity to change the *heart of stone* into a *merciful heart.*

The merciful heart imitates the free generosity of God by giving and sharing, and assuring the brother or sister of our ever-ready help and care. This is the readiness for love and care that people display when they offer the first fruits of the season, the first grapes of their vineyard, to the needy and the poor on the feast of Transfiguration.

λ COSϭIC CELEBRΛΤΙΟN

ΤRANSFIGURATION has a very special attraction which no other feast provides. Besides revealing and celebrating the three essential truths of our Christian religion, namely, the holy Trinity of God, the divinity of our Saviour Jesus Christ, and the divinization of our humanity, it also celebrates our Lord as a perfect Man and perfect God.

Transfiguration has yet another attraction. It is a Cosmic celebration.

When we affirm that God became man, and a part of the universe, we proclaim that the material world is filled with the energies of God. "God is clothed with light", says the psalmist. "God is Light", answers our Blessed Lord, and the Church echoes his voice by saying "the light of Christ illumines the world". The Spirit of glory and of life who reposes in the Son from all eternity has been poured over the universe to divinize it. Even the material world has, therefore, been divinized. It has been renewed in all its elements, in mountains and valleys, in water and in the air we breathe. Saint Gregory of Nazianza writes,

The Trinity has created man according to the divine Image and has placed him in the material world as a 'microcosm' possessing everything that the material world possesses; yet he is destined

for a life in God .... He stands between God and the rest of material creation.

"The material creation is sown in corruption and grows in travail, but it will rise again and be transformed into incorruptibility ..." says Saint Paul.

The material world has fallen into corruption, not because it has sinned, but because we, the intermediary between it and God, have sinned, and have stamped it with our failures. The world is the victim of our sinfulness. Yet it will be redeemed and sanctified by our sanctification, and healed by the radiance of God we shall ourselves reflect upon it. We are the central point of the healing process that is going on between heaven and earth.

The world indeed will rise in glory, and travail will be transformed into beatitude, when Christians will have learned how to contemplate the beauty of the face of Christ, and radiate its brilliance upon the world, to fill it with peace and harmony, and make it shine in glory. Christ is the first and exemplary healer of the universe. He is the Word of God, the Image according to whom not only every human but the whole of creation is made.

Christ reconciled both the human person and the universe by his Incarnation and Redemption. Saint Paul writes again that "Creation waits, in great impatience, the revelation of the children of God" (Rom.8:19).

When the disciples of Christ live the pure love and unconditional forgiveness of their Master and God, the world will be returned to its original state of being a Paradise. Saint Paul seems to intimate this idea when he says: "You are dead and your life is hidden in God with Christ" (Col. 3:3). At the Parousia glory will shine forth from our whole being, and the hidden life of God will become a glory, apparent and shining through the fold of our skin. Just as once glory emanated and shone from the skin and the garments of Christ, and the whole world was filled with beatitude, so it will also radiate from our whole being to fill the world with light, and the cosmos with the glory of redemption.

O Lord, today, on Mount Tabor,
You have manifested the glory of your divinity
to your chosen disciples,
Peter, James and John.

They saw your clothing radiant as light
and your face more brilliant than the sun.
Unable to bear your overwhelming radiance,
or to look upon you,

They fell to the ground and heard a voice
bearing witness from heaven,
'This is my Beloved Son
Who came to the world
to save humanity.'

The Transfiguration of the Lord on the mountain really means that all of life will, one day, be radiant with light and will shine   bright and pure as the sun.   On that day our relationship with God will be luminous and full of beatitude, in our inner soul, as well as in our physical being. Everything around us in this world will also be   full of light and dazzling beauty, as were the vestments of Christ on Mount Tabor.

When David, the forefather of the Lord
foresaw in spirit your coming in the flesh,

he invited the whole creation to rejoice,
crying out prophetically:
O Saviour, Tabor and Hermon shall rejoice
in your name.

Through your Transfiguration,
you returned Adam's nature
to its original splendor,

restoring its very elements
to the glory and brilliance of your divinity.

Wherefore we cry out to you,
the Creator of all:
Glory to you!

Attentive to the cosmic effects of Christ's Transfiguration, the Canon of the feast shows that Christian life is a part of the new creation. It insists on bringing to our attention the idea of rejoicing in God's great works in the universe.

The Canon is indeed a symphony with a special theme repeated again and again, singing of joy, the joy of living and of being in relationship with God and with the material creation. Our liturgical books define joy or rather describe it as that strange welling-up of delight, a tingling near ecstacy in which every sense of our body and soul is like a violin string, making music under the Master's bow. It makes us *sing*; it makes us *clap hands,* it makes us *dance.* It makes us call upon mountains and valleys, upon snow and rain and upon the stars to join in our ecstatic joy.

O Christ,
before your crucifixion,
when you were transfigured
the mountain became a heaven.

A cloud spread and formed a tabernacle.

O You who have spread
the first radiation of light,
to make your works sing in glory,

O Christ their Creator,
direct our ways to your light.

Transfiguration is Christ himself whom we find in every event in our life, in every step we take on our way to the mountain to contemplate his glory. Every doctrine of our Christian religion is a truth bathed in his light and dripping joy and delight from his person. When God became a human face, every human face shone with the light of his Transfiguration.

He who mysteriously spoke to Moses ...
today manifests himself
to his disciples on Mount Tabor

and reveals through his person
that human nature is re-established
in its original splendor.

As witnesses to this grace
and partakers of this joy
He raised up Moses and Elijah
the forerunners of his glorious resurrection.

The Canon transports us from the glory on the mountain to the horror of the cross, and from the defeat of the cross to the triumph of Resurrection, to the communion of saints, to the vision of beauty of the face of Christ bringing before our eyes his presence filled with radiance and love, with life, with goodness and tenderness.

When the liturgy proclaims that in Christ "suffering was wiped out ..." and "death was vanquished by his death ..." it does not mean in the least that suffering and death cease to exist. It teaches with no hesitation or uncertainty that evil will one day turn into beauty, and suffering into glory. Suffering and evil are for the Christian what they were for Christ, instruments for self-realization and occasions to live up to the challenge of divinization.

Because of our divinization, we are able to recognize and face suffering and evil wherever they may be, or however intense, to not criticize or complain about them, but to heal them and so to wipe them out. The Lord ordered us also never to ask *why* evil and suffering exist.   Moses of Judaism, Mohammed of Islam, Buddha and Zarathustra and all other founders of religions tried to explain the cause of suffering and evil; our Blessed Lord did not. When he was asked why there is evil and suffering, his answer was a challenge to cure, heal, and wipe them out. In healing evil and suffering, he said there is *Glory*: "the works of God are displayed" (John 9:3). He then healed the man who was born blind and everyone was amazed!

Suffering and evil cannot break us down, or bend our will to despair. We are made to *carry* any cross with dignity and superb courage. We are not crushed by any burden in life. We see in Transfiguration that reality is greater than appearance. We might look frail and weak, but we know that we have been divinized. Glory is our final destiny.

Creation groans in the Spirit waiting for its proper

transfiguration when everything will be made new (Apoc. 21:5). There will be a new heaven and a new earth (Apoc. 21:1). There will no more be night because the Lord God will be the Light of all (Apoc. 21:23, 22:5).

"The Spirit and the Bride say,

'Come... come, Lord Jesus". (Apoc. 22:17,20).

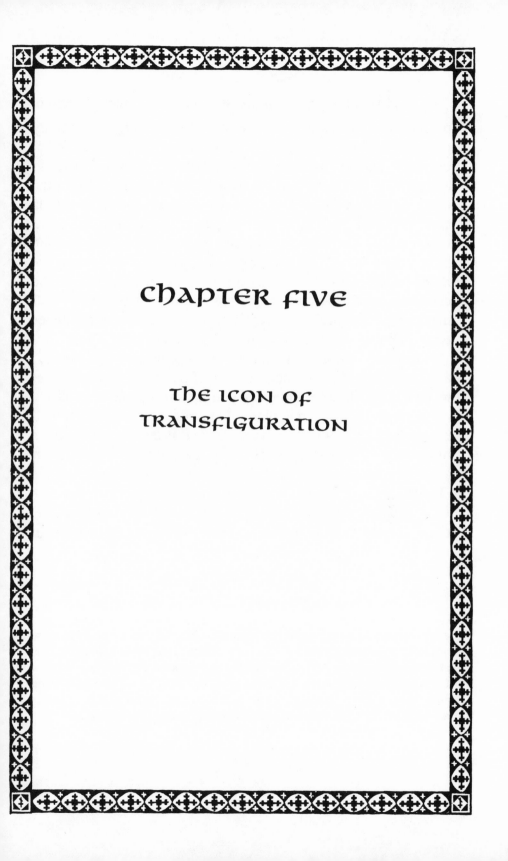

CHAPTER FIVE

THE ICON OF
TRANSFIGURATION

WHAT Christ said and did, theology contemplates in prayer and explains in human words of philosophy, the liturgy proclaims in poetry, and the icon paints in colour. What theology cannot explain or comprehend, liturgy sings in harmonious melodies, and the icon writes in beauty. What the mind cannot grasp by logic, liturgy displays in artistic drama and colourful settings, and the icon represents in silent movements. Theology, liturgy and the icon are a trilogy of the same truth of God. They complete each other. If they are not found together in the performance of the sacraments or the celebrations of the events of the life of Christ, the truth of God may appear magical or unreal. Byzantine tradition combines these three for every sacrament and for every celebration.

After having contemplated Transfiguration in theology, and meditated upon all the grandeur of its beauty in liturgy, let us now study its icon and enter into the movement of its life.

One of the three oldest icons of Transfiguration still extant dates from about the year 600.[1] It is at Saint Catherine's monastery of Mount Sinai. It portrays Transfiguration according to the strictest traditional iconographic laws of the church.

James and John are depicted struck on the ground, overwhelmed by the vision. Their hands are raised in an

---

1. One icon is from the fifth century in Albenga, Northern Italy. It is a symbolic portrayal showing three concentric circles, like waves carrying life and glory, because they emanate from a giant Chi-Rho, the two letters of the name of Christ, symbolizing Christ. This is the oldest. The second is from the time of Emperor Justinian, 549, in St. Apolinarius in Ravenna. This icon portrays Christ in glory, and Moses and Elijah from the waist up. The hand of God points from a cloud, reminding us of the voice of the Father saying: "This is my Beloved ...." Peter, James and John are represented by three sheep.

attitude of consternation. Between the two of them, right at the feet of Christ, is Peter, also cast down and confounded by the light of divinity emanating from the glorified Christ.

It is reported in the Old Testament that both Elijah and Moses responded to the manifestation of God's glory by covering their faces: "Moses hid his face, for he was afraid to look at God" (Ex. 3:6). And when Elijah heard the voice of the Lord coming on the mountain he "wrapped his face in his mantle" (1 Kings 19:13). Likewise, the three disciples are shown covering their faces, because no one in the flesh can bear to gaze upon the glory of divinity.

From the upper center of the icon a bright ray of light descends from heaven upon Christ. This represents God the Father saying: "This is my Beloved Son! Listen to him" (Mark 9:8). The whole mountain seems to be bathed by a luminous mist which is a sign and symbol of the presence of the Holy Spirit.

The icon tells us that Christ is, therefore, more than a prophet, more than a Messiah, and more than any messenger ever sent by God. Christ is God of God, one with the Father and the Spirit. He is surrounded by Moses and Elijah, who are "conversing with him" says the Evangelist Luke, "about his passing away which was soon to happen in Jerusalem" (Luke 9: 31).

Christ stands in all majesty in the center of the icon, right in the middle of an almond-shaped aureole of light surrounding his entire person. The aureole is called *mandorla*, a standard attribute of Christ consisting of a geometrical ellipse, and a zone of light representing the centre of creation. It contains the corruptible universe transformed into a divine milieu, the paradise of Eden where God reposes. This aureole appears mainly in scenes of his Transfiguration and Resurrection, where he is bathed in the light of his divinity.

Mandorla is the normal dwelling place of divinity, a microcosm which only God can penetrate and dwell within. Christ is the centre of convergence between the past, represented by Moses, and the future, represented by Elijah, transcending all creation and seeming to possess all authority in heaven and on earth.

With one hand he imparts a blessing, and with the other he holds a scroll representing the Law and all the Prophets of old. He is Master of the world and the real Maker of the Law. That is why the three Evangelists in unison make us hear the voice of the Father saying: "Listen to him" (Matthew 17:5); "Hear him" in both (Mark 9:7) and (Luke 9:35).

Both Moses and Elijah were found worthy to behold the glory of Christ on Mount Tabor and to be witnesses of his divinity, because in their own life times they both experienced a special theophany of God's glory on other mountains. Both could encounter divine Glory again with their physical eyes without being struck down. In previous encounters they had become sufficiently transfigured to be able now to stand erect beside the divine aura of Christ, and not be consumed by fear. They might touch the mandorla, or be near it to signify that they are called to divinization, but they cannot dwell within its boundaries. Mandorla is only for divinity. Only Christ can reside in it.

MANIFESTATION OF THE TRINITY

WHAT is particularly interesting in the icon of Transfiguration is the fact that it is written as a concrete story, a play in three acts about the manifestation of the Holy Trinity.

Come, O Faithful.
Let us go to the mountain of God,
to the house of our God
that we may see the glory of his Transfiguration
the glory as of the only Son of the Father
receiving Light from Light.

Let us rise through the Spirit
and praise the Consubstantial Trinity
for ever and ever.

Transfiguration is to be the second occasion on which God revealed himself as Trinity of persons. His first revelation was at the Baptism of Christ.

At your Baptism in the river Jordan
O Christ, the worship to the Holy Trinity
    was made manifest.

The voice of the Father bore you witness
    by calling you: "Beloved Son!"

And the Holy Spirit in a form of a dove
confirmed the immutability of this declaration.
O Christ God, O Giver of Light
glory be to You.

The third and final manifestation will probably be at the Parousia, at the end of time, when the Lord "will come to judge the living and the dead".

In the icon of Transfiguration we are present at a gradual unfolding in three successive acts of the mystery of the Trinity.

In the first act, we see that the disciples are present at a real and concrete event of life. There is a ray of light coming down from heaven representing God the Father who gives a resounding testimony of his relationship with Christ. Christ is his Son, i.e., the infinite overflow of his essence, and his Equal: "This is my Beloved Son!" The Son receives the Word and reflects it in brilliance and glory; the Holy Spirit illumines the whole vista with his divine breath, represented by the luminous mist that covers the mountain.

In the second act, the icon depicts the disciples. The three Gospels say that "they fell on their faces", as Moses and Elijah did when they encountered God on other mountains. On one side James covers his eyes. He is on his knees, face down, yet adoring the Incomprehensible. On the other side is John, also on the ground, trying to shield his face with his hands; his shoulders are raised in a gesture of self-protection. Peter is in the middle, down on one hand, the other hand raised towards the figure of Christ. They all adore the Trinity in awesome worship.

In the third act, Moses and Elijah are standing and conversing with the Lord. They are not down because they are already in glory. They are not of this world, yet they are really physically present in this physical world. Moses is more than a prophet. He is a legislator; he holds the scrolls of the Law, yet he is listening to Christ and submitting to him. Elijah is the last precursor of the coming of Christ; Moses is the predecessor. Both Moses and Elijah are wrapped in brilliance, but outside the circle of divine light, and yet near it, signifying that they are called to divinization. Only Christ is in the circle of light. He is the only one essentially divine. The background of the mandorla is a *luminous darkness* to signify the impenetrability of his nature. No human, finite intelligence can comprehend his infinite nature. No eyesight nor intelligence can penetrate this divine darkness of the dwelling place of God.

CbRIST IN GLORY

THE centre of attraction in the icon, and the main object of our attention and worship is Christ standing in glory.

In Christian iconography there are three majestic symbols of the glory of Christ, a circle of light, the nimbus or halo, and the mandorla. The mandorla of Transfiguration is composed of several concentric circles of different shades of deep blue, the central one of which is a luminous dark blue. This darkness signifies that divinity is a mysterious night revealing itself to our intelligence and comprehension only in the measure of our ability to comprehend. These geometrical circles are pierced by rays of light issuing from the body and raiment of Christ to signify that "In him resides all the fullness of the Godhead bodily", as says Saint Paul (Col. 2:9), and from his body, rays are diffused in different strengths and in all directions to signify that we receive the revelation of divinity according to the measure of our spiritual powers.

The mandorla is a song in honour of Christ, proclaiming,

Christ is Glory and Divinity.
He is the Master, Lord and Pantocrator of all!

He is the Light that shines forth
to enlighten every human person in this world.

But in spite of all this glory, the idea of the cross and of the forthcoming passion of Christ are very apparent and clearly represented. The nimbus, or halo around Christ's head in the mandorla is generally in the form of a cross, or quartered by the lines of a cross. It is also sometimes inscribed with three bands to signify his belonging to the Trinity. In the icon of Transfiguration of the famous Mosaics of Ravenna(one of the oldest icons of Transfiguration dating from the sixth century), the whole human form of Christ is replaced by a resplendent, yet simple, cross.

Transfiguration is so important to iconography that iconographers cannot merit the title unless they first produce an icon of Transfiguration according to the most rigorous rules of theology and liturgy. Once they have been recognized as having understood Transfiguration, they are thought to be able to understand any given event of the life of the Lord and any other truth, and consequently they are permitted to write them in colour and beauty. The icon is indeed the privileged place where theology is proclaimed, and liturgy laid out, entirely bathed in the light of Transfiguration. In our monasteries the first rule imposed on iconographers is:

> *To pray with abundant tears*
> *to be all penetrated*
> *by the Light of Transfiguration,*
> *and to seek a holy monk*
> *to chant over them*
> *the hymn of Transfiguration.*

Fidelity to the teaching of Christ will transform them into what the prophecy of Malachi has announced:

> *As for you who look at me*
> *the sun of justice will rise upon you*
> *with my salvation in its rays (Mal. 3:20).*

Saint John translates this promise as: "We shall appear like him when we look at him as he is" (1 John 3:2).

The icon of Transfiguration is the complete revelation of Christ as perfect Man and perfect God. It proclaims that in his humanity the universe is united, renewed, and penetrated by the light of God. In it, divinization is in full view.

As Christ was all light on Tabor, every icon reflects him as light. When viewing or reading an icon one can never say that light comes from below or from above, from sun or moon or stars. In icons there is no other source of light than Christ himself. He is the only Light. His glory, and the brilliance of his divinity, shines forth and penetrates whatever is in the icon - saints and angels, stones and animals. The icon is not simply a representation, it is a realization and a vision that spells *Christ is in glory.*

The Holy Spirit, who illumined the mountain with his *mist*, and covered everyone and everything in this world with brilliance and dazzling beauty, is the same Holy Spirit who illumines *every person coming into this world* and every detail in the icon. He also illumines our vision to see in the icon the whole of creation re-created and renewed. In the icon, creation is redeemed.

DARKNESS OF THE BACKGROUND AND KNOWING GOD

THE background of icons is generally painted in brilliance, a luminous gold, to signify that the icon is in heaven where God resides. In some icons there is a veil like a sheet of clearly impenetrable darkness.[2] This darkness is the sign and symbol that although we can see the human nature of God the Son, we cannot penetrate or comprehend his divine nature. Divine nature is incomprehensible, unknowable, and inexplicable. The only thing we can affirm of God is that *HE IS,* but we shall never know *WHAT HE IS.* This is the veil of darkness behind the figure of Christ in the mandorla. The holy and divine liturgy expresses it in this way:

> *You are God,*
> *beyond description, beyond understanding,*
> *invisible,incomprehensible...*
>
> *always existing, always the same*
> *You and your Only Begotten Son and Your Holy Spirit.*

And Gregory of Nyssa exclaims:

> *Of God we cannot say*
> *but that He Is!*
>
> [And how wonderful it is
> that he is!]

Some Fathers of the Church assert that our knowledge of God develops in three stages. The starting point, and first stage, is his existence. In this stage we know and we affirm that *God is.* Yet he is different and transcendent. This is *illumination.* The second stage is concentration on him and contemplation of him. This is *awareness.* The third stage is a

[2]. Some call it *black.* It is rather a dark blue or dark grey, but never black. Black symbolizes sin and non-existence.

plunging into his mystery, where we come to know that the more we know of him the more we realize that he is *incomprehensible.* His nature is a complete darkness for the human intelligence. God becomes a challenge attracting us more and more, and drawing us ever nearer to him.

In the first stage called *illumination,* we come to know that God is. Consequently, we can establish a living relationship with him; we have a burning desire to come near him and dwell in him. But we realize that our passions stand as a stumbling block in our way to him. They prevent us from concentration. They scatter our attention away from him to *multiplicity,* instead of directing it to *simplicity* - God is the infinitely simple. We then learn that we should not and cannot kill our passions, nor do away with them; we have to learn how to respect them, and cherish them in order to harmonize and synchronize them to unity. They are the necessary tools for our ascension to God and for our contemplation of him.

The second stage is *awareness.* Once we have harmonized our passions we ascend to the second stage in the knowledge of God. Our soul becomes aware that God is awaiting us. We have a "feeling of presence" says Saint Gregory of Nyssa, and of the "indwelling of God within us". He is real and all we say about him is true. Gregory compares this "feeling of presence," or "knowledge" to a "bright cloud like the mist of the holy mountain that overshadows all appearances and slowly guides the soul and accustoms her to look towards him all hidden within the mirror of her inner self" (Commentary on the Canticle).

The third stage *is incomprehensibility of God.*

The more powerful the awareness of the presence of God within us, the more infinitely transcendent will he become. The final result of this awareness is the discovery that he resides in the *darkness of incomprehensibility.* No intellect can comprehend his nature. At this stage, we know *who* he is: Father-Son-Spirit, a superabundance of life and love; but we also know that we shall never know *what* he is!

The luminous darkness in the icon of Transfiguration expresses this *incomprehensibility of God,* or his infinite transcendence, which is an infinite depth that no creature can penetrate or endure. The only comprehensibility that will have a grip on our soul and that will endure forever is the attraction that this mystery will exercise over our insatiable desire to know God more and more.

When the soul comes to realize the incomprehensibility of God she either despairs and gives up the search, or she will go on seeking him, without ceasing, constantly ascending from glory to glory in the luminous night of his nature. It is in this quest that human nature finds its greatest and most perfect satisfaction, its holiness and the credibility to witness to God.

TESTIMONY TO GOD

BECAUSE holiness is the essence of God, every stage of our ascension to God is a *testimony to God.* It makes us his ambassadors and his witnesses.   Even the Law and Commandments are called holy precisely because they give testimony to him.

The Commandments were kept in the Ark called the Ark of testimony and the tabernacle Solomon would build would be called the *dwelling place of Testimony.* God spoke to Moses and said,

> *You must place the throne of mercy*
> *on the top of the Ark.*

Inside the Ark you must place the Testimony
that I shall give you.

There I shall come to meet you (Ex. 25:21,22).

The prophets are called *Carriers of the Testimony of God.* They are all canonized saints in the Byzantine Church and each one has his individual feast day. They were carriers of the Word of God, and consequently, they were holy witnesses to God. The Church recognizes that their proper personality was transfigured by God and his Word. Some theologians thought that they even were divinized.

The faithful witness par excellence was naturally our Blessed Lord himself who is the Word of God. He speaks of what he knows. He witnesses to what he has seen,

I tell you most solemnly
we speak only about what we know
and witness only to what we have seen
(John 3:11).

He reveals the Father because he rests in his embrace,

No one has ever seen God;
it is the only Son who dwells in him
who has made him known (John 1:18).

The perfect and reciprocal intimacy between him and the Father is the deepest level of testimony,

Everything has been entrusted to me
by my Father;

And no one knows the Son
  except the Father,
just as no one knows the Father
  except the Son,
and those to whom
the Son chooses to reveal him (Matthew 11:27).

Testimony is communion between the witness and his source of life. It is the love he or she has for God in obedience to his will. Christ was the perfect exemplary of witness and of obedience. The Apostles who have received from Christ are his witnesses. It is for this reason that after the death of Judas Iscariot, Peter asked the other apostles to replace him by another one who had seen and experienced, and who could carry on the witness,

We must choose someone
who has been with us
the whole time that the Lord Jesus
was travelling around with us.

Someone who was with us
right from the time when John was baptizing
until the day when he was taken up
from us.

And he can act with us as a witness
to his resurrection (Acts 1:21-23).

Having been with the Lord is the source of the testimony and witness to his victory. For this reason the contemplation of Christ is called *bios apostolikos* (apostolic life). Only the one who lives with Christ can be sent as a witness.

chapter six

the spirituality of
transfiguration

ASCENT TO TRANSFIGURATION

OUR Fathers in the faith found a special challenge and a special joy in commenting on four steps that lead us to the mountain of Transfiguration where we could contemplate the beauty of the face of our Lord, and share in the splendor of his divinity. The first step of ascent to Christ is purification, the second is prayer, the third is contemplation. The summit and crowning of this ascent of spiritual life is illumination.

These four steps are not mechanically established, that we can move forward to the next step only when we have first perfected the one before it. All four are intermingled. We go from one to the other naturally, spontaneously, and freely, according to our present psychological and spiritual condition. We can enjoy moments of illumination while still struggling with our sins and failures, and we can go back to spiritual warfare after having attained the summit of glory in contemplation.

FIRST STEP: PURIFICATION

SAINT Basil says: "When he saw that man was made in the image and likeness of God, the devil realized that it was useless for him to fight against God, so instead he entangled God's image in evil."

The evil consists in forgetting the image and likeness of God, and abandoning one's self to the fascination of becoming one's own God where we only see our present interests and our own life-style, forgetting the relationship that unites us to God and to the other.

The image of God is not destroyed by sin but concealed and paralyzed by it. Sin does not take away from our soul its original form, but puts on top of it a foreign element that covers it and confuses it. Confusion hides the original beauty, but does not blot it out. In sin the mind is distracted, the imagination obscured, and our intelligence becomes distorted and cannot see its divine reality in God. The warfare is between the spirit of God who inhabits us and harmonizes our faculties, and the enemy - the deceit, the pretence, the hypocrisy and self-centredness of our passions which disturb and scatter.

The struggle is a struggle for purification and for a return to our original beauty, the image of God in us. It is for the recovery of our pristine dignity and clarity of the likeness of God. We must bury the old man Adam, our selfishness and isolation, and rise with Christ to the new man of love and harmony. Christ indeed came not only to raise up our flesh but to save his image and likeness as well.

Division and isolation are the characteristics of the flesh which are the elements of division, while the image and likeness harmonizes and unites: "Awake you who sleep, and arise from the dead, and Christ shall give you light" (Eph. 5:14). Awakening to the light of God is to perceive our true self, a divine art, requiring dedication and ceaseless attention, constant vigilance, and great generosity of heart. The battle for purification is a battle of life and death for which our true self is the prize.

Purification is not, therefore, a free gift of nature, but a courageous fight which can be won only by incessant asceticism and prayer. We ascend to Transfiguration by prayer, the first steps of purification by which we gather our faculties of imagination and intellect into a wholeness where our heart will find repose and harmony. Prayer is the matrix of spiritual life, and the key to the Kingdom of our inner peace and harmony.

SECOND STEP: PRAYER

THE first step of the ascension of Mount Tabor for the contemplation of the beauty of the face of Christ is purification. The second step is prayer.

Saint Luke associates the event of Transfiguration with prayer. He writes that prior to the event of Transfiguration, "One day when the Lord was praying alone ... he put a question to his disciples". It was this question that caused Peter to proclaim the Lord to be "the Christ, the Son of the living God" (Luke 9:20) and to ascend the mountain. The Fathers of the Church and our deep rooted tradition hold that prayer is indeed of primary importance and essential for the building up of spiritual life and for the ascension of the mountain of God. Our Lord himself is shown in the Gospel to be our Model as a perfect Leader of prayer.

When only twelve years old the Lord "went to the temple to pray" (Luke 2:41). The first theophany of God was made manifest at his baptism "when he was in prayer" (Luke 3:21). And again before he chose the twelve, he went up the mountain "and he spent the whole night in prayer" (Luke 6:12).

Only in prayer can we experience the indwelling of God; only in prayer can we envision the divine light, and comprehend our divinization; only prayer can sustain us on the road to Christ. "He who is in prayer," says Evagrius, "is all wrapped in the light of God. He is the dwelling place of God."

Praying is not merely saying words to tell God what he does not know, or to remind him of things he has forgotten. Praying is the search for the God we have forgotten, and for the

96

voice we are wont to hear. The spoken words we utter in prayer are only tools we use to become aware of God's presence and to express our relation of loving him and belonging to him. The power of words derives from the authority of the original Word, Christ, who is the Word of God. The Lord said, "I have given them your word" (John 17:14); and again, "Ask and it shall be given you ... how much more shall your Father in heaven give the Holy Spirit to those who ask him" (Luke 11: 9-13). He urges us to "ask" which means to use words in our prayer. "If you abide in me, and my word abides in you, you shall ask what you will, and it shall be done to you" (John 15:7). When asked to teach his disciples a method for praying - "Lord, teach us how to pray" - the Lord did not give them a method, or a theory on prayer, but words to be said. And the words the Lord gave us to say are enshrined in a poem-like form of infinite dimensions that enlarge the heart and imagination of the human person to the immensity of the universe. The "Our Father, Abba Abenoo" is a dreamland of beauty and security, where the earth and life on earth become a heaven and where love and forgiveness reign supreme.

It is not by our own force that our words have effect, but by faith in the unseen God, Source of all power and of all goodness. Our words are the gift of our human personality left upon the altar of God. They are the gift of our mind which is enlightened by its supreme Object, God who is Source and End of all reality and knowledge and expression of knowledge. This awareness of his presence is so essential that the heart of prayer is not the word itself, but the faith, contrition, self-surrender to the Lord that the word contains. We can even stand before the Lord without any words, and it will still be prayer.

Saint Basil recommends four actions to be included in prayer. He tells us to *first glorify God, then give thanks to him for his goodness and love, then confess your sins to be forgiven and finally ask him to grant you what you need for your soul and body ....* " *"The power of prayer"*, says Saint Gregory Palamas, *"performs and accomplishes the actual resurrection of man and his union with God"* in divinization.

The saying of Evagrius on theology has become the saying of our monks, written on every monk's cell, "A theologian is one who prays and only he who prays is theologian." Another saying, and still the most important advice given to those who come to seek the monastic way of life, is: "No one can ever know God if God does not reveal himself to him or her in prayer."

The basic principle of the Christian way of life is that persons are made for prayer, and there is no activity more natural to them. Prayer is the very breath of life God placed in human persons, making living souls out of the dust of creation (Gen. 2:7). Even without the formal knowledge of God, all human activity is prayer through the indwelling of the Holy Spirit. All transforming activity is an attachment to God.

Metropolitan Dimitri of Rostov gives this superb description of prayer:

> *As a flame increases when it is constantly fed, so prayer, made often, with the mind dwelling ever more deeply in God, arouses divine love in the heart. And the heart, set on fire, will warm the inner man, will enlighten and teach him, revealing to him all its unknown and hidden wisdom, and making him like a flaming seraph, always standing before God within his spirit, always looking at him within his mind, and drawing from this vision the sweetness of spiritual joy.*

Third step: Contemplation

In our ascent to Transfiguration, after purification and prayer comes the third step, contemplation.

The more conscious we become of the reality of God, the more watchful our heart will grow, and the more capable we will become of seeing the image and likeness of God in ourselves and in others. The more we see what is beautiful in ourselves, in others, and in nature, the more joy and beauty we will encounter and experience. Saint Basil says: "As things that are transparent become very bright and radiate brightness and light when they are penetrated by light, so are those who carry the Holy Spirit and are illuminated by him. They become spiritual, and, in turn, they will radiate grace and joy." They become *contemplatives*.

There is a centuries-old tradition in our Christian culture that tells the story of the foetus in the womb. Our mothers treasure it from generation to generation, and they tell with great delight how angels bathe the foetus every day in the brilliance of the beauty of Christ's face, and unravel to him or her the marvels of the universe in order to prepare it for contemplation.

They say that infants smile at any face because in the face they recognize the brilliance of the face of Christ they contemplated in the womb. They abandon themselves to the arms that stretch to them because they recognize the image and likeness of God they have already seen while in the womb. Glory leaps up from their inner soul to meet the glory of Christ even in the faces of the most wretched of criminals. They delight in every movement of life with wonder and awe because they live again the experience given them by the angels in the womb.

It was only after having contemplated the brightness of God in the human face of the divine Infant in Bethlehem that angels sang glory to the whole universe:

Glory to God in heaven!
Peace upon the earth!
And harmony among nations!

The often repeated saying of our Byzantine monks was "You become what you contemplate."

Contemplating beauty naturally increases our consciousness of the beauty that exists in the world. For to the one whose mind is steeped in the glory of God, every-day incidents reveal special joys, and every person we encounter becomes a special delight.

Abouna Bechara of the Salvatorians was a shining master of spirituality. His constant teaching was that he who contemplates God will reflect strength of character; and a soul that sees the inner realities of Christ perceives the inner beauty of every human person. For him there was nothing mean or trivial in creation. He experienced the energies of God shining through everything and every person, and saw loveliness everywhere. Abouna Bechara lived in contemplation lit by the light of Transfiguration.

Teilhard de Chardin has said: "Jesus Christ is shining diaphanously through the whole world to those who have eyes to see." And in the words of William Blake, "if the doors of perception were cleansed, everything will appear to man as it is, INFINITE."

There is a special icon called "the unexpected joy". The mother of God is holding Christ, who has discovered a shining pearl within a handful of mud. He admires its brilliance and shows much pride in its beauty. The Mother looks at him and radiates the delight of a great surprise mixed with reverence. This signifies that even in the most miserable situations, and in the most seemingly wretched people, contemplation will discover a "special pearl" dripping with beauty and joy. This is the "unexpected joy" that only contemplation can produce.

Anyone contemplating beauty is bound to feel beautiful and clean. Those who expose themselves to sadness will become sad, and will feel heavily burdened. The artist will see harmony and beauty everywhere, and the musician, sounds of life and balance in every movement. This is a law that applies as well to spiritual life. The more we contemplate the face of Christ, the more joy and beauty we shall encounter in the world, in ourselves and in other people. Deep down within us, imperceptible brightness will grow.

The way we interpret things and persons will point to the stuff of which we are really made. If we see beauty, it means that our inner eye is beautiful. If we see ugliness we may be sure ugliness is dwelling in the recesses of our soul. The Lord our God, said in the Gospel: "The mouth speaks of the abundance of the heart ... The light of the body is the eye: if therefore thine eye be clear, thy whole body shall be full of light ..."(Matthew 6:22).

Thomas Merton illustrates this process of contemplation in his autobiography the "Seven Story Mountain." Merton left the world for the monastery because he was disgusted with the world, where he could find only ugliness, sin, and disorder. He found a bad taste in everything he encountered in the world. But after seven years of prayer and contemplation in the monastery he happened to go back to the world. Here is what he wrote concerning that visit:

I met the world and found it no longer so

wicked after all. Perhaps the things I resented about the world when I left it were defects of my own that I had projected upon it.

Now, on the contrary, everything stirred me with a deep and mute sense of compassion.I seemed to have lost an eye for merely exterior detail and to have discovered, instead, a deep sense of love and pity for the souls that such details never fully reveal. I went through the city, realizing for the first time in my life how good are all the people in the world and how much value they have in the sight of God.

God is the source and the final purpose of the whole of creation. When we contemplate him we see him as he is. He is beautiful, beauty is his essence, and beauty becomes delight in every aspect of life.

Christ, our God, identified himself with every human face; *Whatever you have done to these little ones,* he said, *you have done it to me!* Once we have contemplated the face of Christ, we cannot help but see our brother and sister as beautiful as Christ himself. It is in the brother and sister that we experience, see, feel, hear, touch, smell, and taste the presence of God. Saint Isaac writes:

> *When we can see that all human persons are good and none is impure, we can then be sure that we are pure of heart... When you see your brother falling into sin cover him with the mantle of your love .*

We talk about our relation to God and to our brothers

and sisters in words of actions and sensations because this is the only way that renders the experience of God real, and our uniqueness true. God is directly and immediately being *sensed, seen, loved,* and *served* in others. As we see the beauty of the face of Christ in them, we see our own uniqueness, and we experience the uniqueness of every other creature, even in the seemingly most rejected and despised.

One of the strictest and hardest spiritual writers, Saint John Climacus, writes in his *Ladder of Perfection:*

> *I know a man who, when he saw a woman of great beauty, praised the Creator. The sight of her lit within him the love of God and from his eyes gushed a flood of tears. It was a wondrous thing to behold. What would have been a sadness of heart for another becomes for him a crown of victory.*

"Those who have contemplated the beauty of the face of Christ become all fire", says Simeon the New Theologian; and he adds: "They can even transmit their inner radiance through their own physical bodies just as physical fire transmits its effects to iron" (Discourse 83).

Iron is transformed into fire. It is purified and becomes one with fire, yet it remains iron. In contemplating beauty the human person becomes transfigured into beauty and radiates beauty. The radiance of Christ in the human person does not destroy or take away anything from the human. It becomes in humans a flame of love so intense that they can develop into a merciful heart.

"What is a merciful heart?", inquires Saint Isaac the

Syrian. And he answers:

> *It is a heart that burns with love*
> *for the whole creation,*
> *for men, for birds, for beasts,*
> *even for demons, and for every creature.*
>
> *When a man, with such a heart as this,*
> *thinks of the creatures or looks at them,*
> *his eyes are filled with tears.*
>
> *An overwhelming compassion*
> *makes his heart grow small*
> *and weak and he cannot endure*
> *to hear or see any suffering, even the smallest pain,*
> *inflicted upon any creature.*
>
> *Therefore he never ceases to pray with tears*
> *even for the irrational animals,*
> *for the enemies of truth,*
> *and for those who do him evil,*
> *asking that they may be guarded*
> *and may receive God's mercy.*
>
> *And for the reptiles also he prays*
> *with a great compassion,*
> *which rises up endlessly in his heart*
> *until he shines again and is glorious*
> *bathed in the glory of God (Sermon 48).*

Paul the Hermit, one of the Desert Fathers, used to say:

> *"When a man obtains a merciful heart*
> *all things become subject to him, even wild animals, just*

like to Adam in paradise
before the fall" (Apophthegmata of the fathers.)

Some marvelous stories are told about the Fathers of the desert, as they were told later on about some saints in the Western Church (such as Saint Francis), whose clarity of heart exercised power to make even wild animals obey them.

FOURTh STEP: ILLUMINATION

AFTER purification, prayer and contemplation comes the fourth and highest degree of spiritual life, illumination.

Illumination is the transformation into the light of Transfiguration. The Fathers and theologians of the Eastern Church have always seen a connection between the illumination of Tabor and the future vision of God in heaven. Saint Gregory of Nazianza defines illumination as:

> *A rapture of glory coming out of the Trinity*
> *to capture all the powers of the intelligence,*
> *and penetrate all the senses of our nature.*
> *It liberates them from the tendency of*
> *being scattered in different directions,*
> *and concentrates them into one and unique*
> *object which is the Trinity.*

Once illuminated by the contemplation of the Trinity we can experience the fullness of meaning of our baptism, and of the grace of divinization. We move out of our existential darkness and our self-centeredness, to enter into the light of the disciples saw on Mount Tabor. It is not the vision of the nature of God, which is an absolute impossibility even to angels, but a perception of the Uncreated Energy that comes from God, and penetrates our nature with light and grace. Only God can reveal God; the Holy Spirit unites us with the Son and through the Son we go to the Father and we know him. The experience of the presence of God is a real knowledge, where the impossible becomes a reality and the invisible a tangible experience. It is like the "sleep" the disciples experienced. They were all wrapped up in sleep yet they kept fully awake. They were completely unconscious of the world around them, yet they knew it was there, real and true, and God was there as true and real.

For Saint Simeon the New Theologian, the knowledge of God is not obtained any more in the darkness of the cloud as for Moses on Mount Sinai but in the luminous light of Transfiguration:

> *In contemplation, the saint asks God;*
> *Are you my God? 'and the answer comes,*
> *'Yes, I am the God who became man for you,*
> *and behold it is I who made you,*
> *and will make you again god....'*
> *The light of God becomes in us as luminous*
> *as the sun*
> *in the splendor of its zenith*
> *and the soul realizes that it also is in*
> *the center of light*
> *all penetrated by joy and overwhelmed with*
> *tears....*
> *It feels also that the light sticks*
> *in a manner beyond understanding to*
> *our very flesh and slowly penetrates our limbs ...*

thus transforming us into fire and light...

The knowledge of God is the experience of him as our light and the very breath of our life.

Nil Sorsky (1508) the monk who introduced Byzantine hesychasm to Russia, explains how the Uncreated Energy works in the one who is caught up in the vision of God:

> *When the soul undergoes spiritual activity*
> *and subjects itself to God it is enlightened ...*
> *by an intense light.*
>
> *The mind experiences a feeling of joy*
> *similar to the perfect joy*
> *that awaits us in the life to come.*
>
> *When an undescribable sweetness warms the heart,*
> *and the whole body feels its repercussion.*
> *Man lays aside all disorder of passion*
> *and becomes oblivious of life itself*
> *to realize that the Kingdom of heaven*
> *consists of nothing other than this ecstatic state.*
>
> *He experiences that the Love of God*
> *is sweeter than life itself*
> *and the knowledge of God sweeter than honey ...."*
> (G.A. Maloney, *The Breath of the Mystic*).

This is the beatific "sleep" the disciples experienced on Mount Tabor.

In Byzantine spirituality three saints have been called "Theologian", precisely because they seem to have experienced such an illumination. The Apostle and Evangelist John, Saint

Gregory of Nazianza, and Saint Simeon, who, because he lived in a later period, was called "new theologian".

Simeon lived in the tenth century, and probably died in 1022. He gave us a classical description of illumination as he himself experienced it. This experience might have been similar to the one the disciples experienced on Mount Tabor. Saint Simeon writes:

I see a light which is not of this world.

Sitting in my cell, I see within me
the Maker of the world.

I converse with him and I love him,
and I feed on this one divine Image.
United with him I am raised to the heavens.
Where is my body now? I do not know
For God has loved me.

God received me into his very being
and he hides me in his embrace.
I am in heaven and at the same time
in my own heart.
God becomes visible to me.
The Ruler of all appears to me
in a way like he does to angels,
yet in a way more precious.

To them he is invisible and unapproachable
while to me he is visible
and he unites himself with my being.

It is this state that Saint Paul described
when he said:
that 'eye had not seen nor ear heard.'

Being in this state,
I do not have any desire to leave my cell.
But I long to hide myself
in a deep hole in the ground
and there, removed from the upper world,
I would gaze on my immortal Lord
and Creator'
(G.A.Maloney, *The Breath of the Mystic).*

From these testimonies of saints we learn that this high level of contemplation produces in them a supernatural transfiguration where they are as in a deep sleep, yet fully awake.   In this state of illumination they also bear a resemblance to Christ on the mountain. They radiate beatitude. Quite often Abouna Bechara of the Salvatorians radiated such a brilliance of heavenly illumination that his fellow monks and brothers were overwhelmed with joy and an ineffable peace merely at the sight of him.

It is this transfiguration that is described in the famous "conversation" between Saint Seraphim of Sarov and Nicholas Motovilov, his disciple.

Seraphim and Motovilov were walking in the forest on a wintry day talking about the need one has to acquire the Holy Spirit. This led Motovilov to ask his spiritual father how a man can know with certainty that he is "in the Spirit of God." Father Seraphim took him very firmly by the shoulders and said:

My Son, we are both at this moment in the Holy Spirit.

Why don't you look at me?

I cannot look, Father,
because your eyes are flashing like lightning.
Your face has become brighter than the sun
and it hurts my eyes to look at you.

'Don't be afraid' he said.
At this very moment
you have yourself become
as bright as I am.
You are yourself in the fullness
of the Spirit of God
at this moment.
Otherwise you would not be able to see me as you do ...

But why, my Son, why don't you look me in the eyes?
Just look, and don't be afraid;
the Lord is with us.

"After these words," continues Motovilov,

I glanced at his face,
and there came over me an even greater reverent awe.

Imagine in the center of the sun,
in the dazzling light of its mid-day rays,
the face of a man talking to you!

You see the movement of his lips
and the changing expression of his eyes
and you hear his voice,
you feel someone holding your shoulders,
yet you do not see his hands,

you do not even see yourself or his body
but only a blinding light
spreading far around
for several yards
and lighting up with its brilliance the snow blanket
which covers the forest glade
and the snow flakes which continue to fall unceasingly.
(Seraphim de Sarov, Entretien avec Motovilov -
Bellefontaine No. 11).

ThE "fEAR Of GOD"

THE result of illumination is a peaceful rest in that "hole in the ground" of St. Simeon, or the brilliance of the transfigured face of Abouna Bechara. Brilliance shines but does not blind. The Evangelists translate this experience as *a sleep* or *fear*. This peaceful fear is indeed the characteristic reaction of man in the presence of the divine, the awesome and wonderful, inseparable from illumination.

In our human relationships the deeper the rapture of love, the more sublime is its illumination and the more penetrating is the *fear* that it engenders. Indeed, the real rapture of love always inspires a mixture of desire and fear. The desire is to secure the union with the beloved, and the fear is that very feeling which springs from the sublime grandeur of this union, the fear of losing it. This fear is not a pain, nor any unpleasant sensation, but an incalculable pleasure of triumph and glory, mixed with disappointment in one's own limitations, a strange mixture of contrasts, that makes us tremble and be overwhelmed by something greater than ourselves. We are afraid of ourselves realizing that we are capable of losing, or degrading the object of our Love. The vision of the beauty of Christ, like the rapture of love, is of such beatitude that we long for it to last forever. "Lord," said Peter, "it is wonderful for us to be here. Let us make here three tabernacles; one for You and one for Moses, and one for Elijah" (Matthew 17:2).

The liturgy commands insistently such sentiment of fear in the presence of God:

> Let us stand well! Let us stand in fear!
> Let us be attentive ...
> With fear of God approach to the Eucharist ..."
> O Lord, nail our very flesh with the fear of you
> so that looking on you at all times
> and guided by the light that shines from you,
> we may behold the unapproachable eternal light
> and unceasingly address to you,
> Eternal Father,
> and to your only Begotten Son
> and to your all holy, good and life-giving Spirit
> our thanksgiving and worship...

We should note again that the four stages of spiritual life, as described here, are not fixed stations where one is bound, and from which one cannot escape until perfected. Anyone who enters into a dialogue of love may move freely from one stage to the other. A person who has attained to illumination may sometimes find himself or herself struggling with self-centredness and selfishness. And the beginner in spiritual life, and even the sinner, may experience the beatitude of heaven and sometimes soar to the highest degree of contemplation.

All of us, the perfect and the beginner, may move back and forth, up and down, from one level of experience to another, according to our personal, physical and psychological situations, to our availability to the inspiration of God, and to our faithfulness to the exercise of asceticism.

CONCLUSION: MYSTICAL MEANING OF TRANSFIGURATION

IN his sermon on the eve of Transfiguration, Saint Athanasius of Sinai summarizes all the spiritual benefits of the feast of Transfiguration by saying:

> *Yes, today the Lord has been seen on the mountain;*
> *the nature of Adam has been restored*
> *to its former beauty,*
> *to the image and resemblance of God,*
> *after having been obscured by sin.*
>
> *Today, our nature has been transformed*
> *and lit with the brilliant rays of divinity*
> *after having been lost on the mountains*
> *where idolatry prevailed.*
>
> *Today has donned a divine vestment*
> *wrapped in light as with a mantle,*
> *he who had put on himself*
> *the skin of our humanity.*
>
> *Today, on the mountain of Tabor*
> *has appeared as by a miracle*
> *the reality of future life*
> *and of the Kingdom of joy.*

Today, the heralds of the Old
and of the New Testaments
gather in a marvelous way around God
carrying astonishing mysteries.

Today, on Mount Tabor,
the mystery of the Cross has been revealed.
As He was crucified between two thieves
on the Mount of the Skull,
the Lord has appeared in all his divinity
between Moses and Elija ....

And again he sounds the final hymn of triumph by saying:

The celebration of Transfiguration
  is a mixture of joy
and of lightheartedness.

The people who gather to honour the feast
  that took place on the divine mountain
sing in unison with one heart and one mind
together with the angels.

The assembly dances with the stars,
  proclaims with the apostles,
  prophesies with Moses,
  clamors with Elijah
  and makes revelations
  from the roof-tops of mountains.

We thunder in the clouds
and to the heavens we give our testimony.
We sound the trumpet on the rock
and convoke Nazareth,

and summon Galilee
to join in the feast.

We brighten the feast,
and adorn it with praises.

We dance with the mountains
and intone melodies with young maidens
In honour of the real God, our God,
Our Lord and Saviour Jesus Christ.

Transfiguration is not simply an event out of the two-thousand-year old past, or a future yet to come. It is rather a reality of the present, a way of life available to those who seek and accept Christ's nearness.

Once we are attuned to the beauty that radiates from the face of Christ we become free, and we can free others. Once at peace with ourselves we can create peace in the heart of others. Because we are penetrated by the light of Christ and the brilliance of his divinization we can brighten the world.

We acknowledge the goodness of everything and of everyone because we ourselves are full of goodness. We contemplate goodness; we cherish it and dwell in it; and we become what we contemplate.

To celebrate Transfiguration is to implant in our soul a merciful heart, a graceful movement of life made of wonder and amazement. With it we appreciate life, love life, and we are thankful for life. It is a joy, a rest, and a supreme security to possess a merciful heart.

To celebrate Transfiguration is to love and to forgive as God himself loves and forgives. It is to be perfect as our Father in heaven is perfect.

We proclaim peace and love because we know that we are loved. We carry our tired brothers and sisters, the suffering, the sick, and the disappointed, because we are soaked in the peace of Christ. We provide joy because Christ in us is our source of joy.

Our inspiration comes from above. It comes from the radiance shining through the transfigured Christ.

When we go on
discovering and admiring,
and playing the noble game of life,
we are in Transfiguration.

When we feast in wonder and praise
we live in Transfiguration.
When we display vitality and hope
we radiate Transfiguration.

When women and men become fully alive
they are with Christ on Mount Tabor
bathed in Transfiguration.

To Christ our Lord God and Saviour
who was transfigured on Mount Tabor
be honour and glory
for ever and ever.
Amen.

ICON OF TRANSFIGURATION

Most details of the scene of Transfiguration usually shown in icons are represented in this one. There are three mountain tops, and Christ stands on the middle one, Tabor; Elijah on the right, on Mount Horeb; Moses on the left, on Mount Sinai.

Christ is all in snow-white garments standing in the Mandorla of divinity. The pale blue at the edge of the Mandorla gradually darkens into dark blue, almost into black in the centre to signify the "unknowability of God whose divine nature is impenetrable".

The three apostles are on the slope of the mountain right in the centre. They have been struck by the light emanating from Christ. John has fallen and he covers his face, blinded by the splendor of Christ. St. James leans his head on his hand and covers his eyes. St. Peter kneels down and at the same time he lifts up his hands towards Christ as if speaking to him: "Lord, it is good to be here!"

At left centre, the Lord and his disciples are going up the mountain. Further right centre is the descent of warning not to tell anyone of the vision until after the Resurrection.